MW01680458

The FROG Effect Workbook:

TOOLS AND STRATEGIES TO FOREVER RECOGNIZE OTHERS' GREATNESS

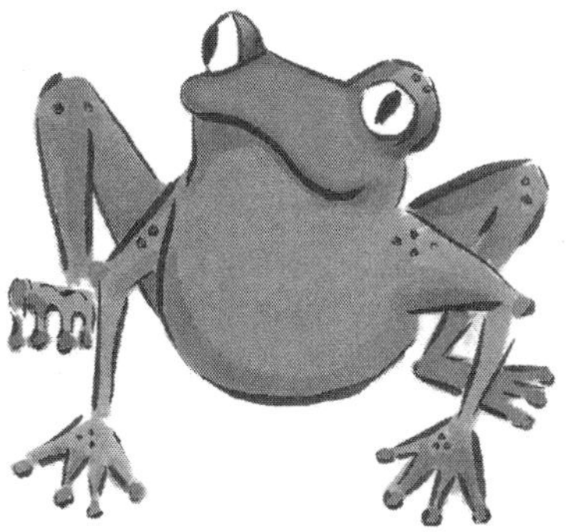

By:
Sarah McVanel &
Brenda Zalter-Minden

The FROG Effect Workbook
Tools And Strategies To Forever Recognize Others' Greatness

ISBN: 978-0-9951572-0-0

Printed in Canada

Introduction

Here's the Point....

You spend more waking hours at work than you do anywhere else. But are you really awake?

Most of us spend part or huge segments of our careers disengaged, unmotivated, and even resentful; we focus on the time and energy our work and people *take* from us - our bosses, our coworkers, and our staff. It doesn't have to be this way. This workbook is packed with tools, ideas and suggestions to help you **get powerful at work that will forever leave you feeling resourceful and inspired.** In fact, the strategies are so universal you can bring them into other facets of your life as well.

This workbook is designed to build on and address the unmet need for proven practical applications; we've heard from readers of our first book, *Forever Recognize Others' Greatness: Solution Focused Strategies for Satisfied Staff, High Performing Teams and Healthy Bottom Lines*, that they would like clear "how to's" in order to get the results that we promise can be realized. You will notice that the structure of this workbook follows the same chapter titles and focus of our original book. We hope this provides ease of application and inspiration!

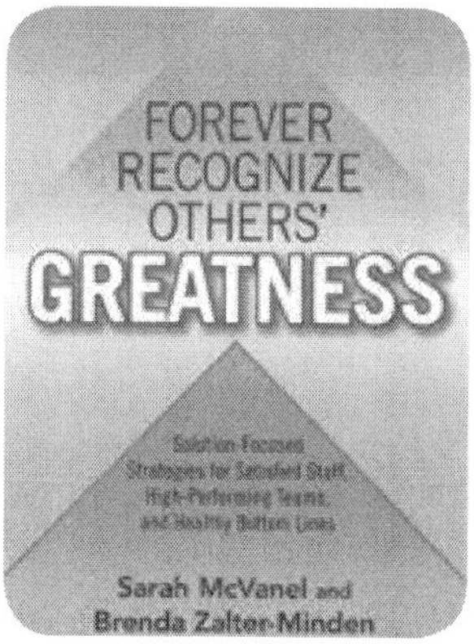

Trainers, facilitators, therapists, and mediators will immediately see the benefit of broadening their toolkit with new energizing solution focused exercises. Leaders too will be inspired to incorporate the tools in a whole host of ways - in team meetings, planning sessions, one-on-one meetings and more. In other words, we have created this workbook for you *and* for the teams and organizations. Share, build on and experiment with the ideas presented here, and you no doubt will come up with your own versions that enrich the experience by aligning to what works in your unique environment.

> **BONUS!**
>
> **Downloadable tools, templates and even watch videos! Do even more and stay inspired by visiting**
>
> **www.f-r-o-g.ca**
>
> 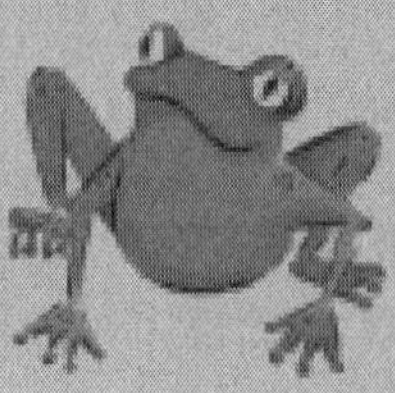

Why is this so important...now?

We are in the midst of a talent shortage that shows no signs of easing until 2030. To keep your top talent, you will need to continually seek ways to build motivation, ingenuity, and commitment within the workplace to keep the talent you already have; **organizations' greatest asset - its people - walk out the door every night and can choose whether or not to come back the next day.** If they do return, they can decide how much discretionary energy, creativity, and knowledge they will contribute. Recruiters are calling your people; LinkedIn job ads are waiting in their inboxes; visions of sabbaticals to far off places are dancing in their heads and fantasies of starting their own business from home are possibilities that your top talent may be entertaining at any given time. Wouldn't it be wise to incorporate strategies into your workplace that provides the insulation needed during times of talent scarcity?

You can help to ensure your organization remains your top talent's preferred option. By **continually building a dynamic culture where everyone can do their best work.** If you need inspiration or new ideas about how to do just that, we're thrilled you picked up this workbook and promise your solutions are here.

This workbook is full of the tools required to bring a FROG™ lens - Forever Recognize Others' Greatness - to life by providing our top four to seven exercises for each section. For each exercise, we share a story of how it has been used successfully, explain the benefits, outline the tools required, and offer a variety of ways to adapt the exercises for maximum flexibility in your work settings. You will soon see by experimenting with these tools how they enable you and your colleagues to get curious, be brave and intentional about tapping into their own greatness and elevating it in others.

In the true spirit of FROG, we have to acknowledge someone who has been our rock through the creation of both books and our editor of this workbook, Sandeep Aujla. Sandeep, we are indebted to you for sharing your extensive knowledge of psychology, experience in adult education, and gifts as a facilitator. We all have benefited from your talents!

Thank-you to all the authors and colleagues who gave us permission to publish exercises and advice. We are a stronger community when we share our knowledge and we come from a generous community indeed. For that reason we are also grateful to our clients for allowing us to share their success stories. We want to FROG you for your dedication to living the true spirit of recognition and commend you for the incredible results you are getting!

Look for more resources including free downloadable tools and even more exercises at www.f-r-o-g.ca. You can also reach out to use through our websites www.greatnessmagnified.com (Sarah) and www.bzmsolutions.com (Brenda). Please share your experiences of what worked, how you modified what we've provided here, and what your results are. Let's build a community of workplace greatness!

Oh, and by the way, we've alluded to it anyway but it's worth mentioning again. This stuff works on your family too! Family gatherings will never be the same again! Enjoy!

Sarah & Brenda

TABLE OF CONTENTS

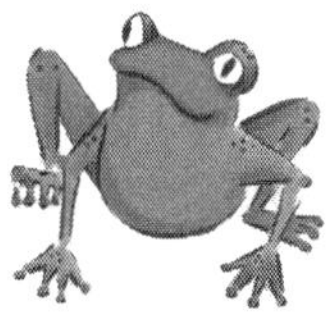

CHAPTER ONE

The Power of Finding Solutions vs. Solving Problems

"Begin doing what you want to do now. We are not living in eternity. We have only this moment, sparkling like a star in our hand -- and melting like a snowflake."
—Francis Bacon Sr.

Our best hope for this chapter is to review the essential tenets of the solution focused approach through a variety of interactive, educational and stimulating exercises. We intend these exercises to be generic and accessible to all as they reinforce the strengths that can be found in any person, team or organization. The exercises emphasize some of the essential tenets of the solution focused approach such as the need to listen differently, how to get a subjective read on where people are at through scaling, and the art of complimenting.

Exercise

1. Listen, Build, Select

While training a group of staff at the *York Centre* (Richmond Hill, Ontario) about how to understand the difference between problem solving and solution building, we created this exercise based on Peter DeJong and Insoo Kim Berg's instruction to **listen** to what a person is saying, **build** on what they are saying by **selecting** certain words and phrases using the person's language while emphasizing their talents, passions and virtues. Following the exercise, people were surprised to hear the many different paths someone could take in formulating their next comment or question from hearing a simple phrase. They became more aware of the impact we can have in shaping a conversation in one direction or another by staying focused on exceptions, strengths and coping strategies.

This exercise is great because it:

- Helps people understand the notion of positive hypothesizing
- Encourages people to listen differently for talents, passions and virtues
- Allows people to hear and discover multiple ways we can respond in any conversation
- Provides a new platform for moving conversations away from problems towards solutions

Materials:

- Any script of a dialogue, report or case study depicting the topic you are discussing that you would like to explore differently

Instructions:

1. Divide the participants into groups of four or five
2. Explain the purpose of the exercise which is to determine the next statement or question they would say or ask once they hear the first comment
3. Ask the volunteer to read the first statement
4. Encourage each participant to write down how they would respond before discussing it aloud
5. People then share their statements and the volunteer decides which one she or he likes best to move the conversation in the best direction
6. The volunteer then reads the next statement from the script
7. Repeat two or three times
8. Debrief

Debriefing Questions:

There are two sets of debriefing questions for this exercise:

Starting with the volunteer:

1. *What did you notice?*
2. *Which statements did you prefer?*
3. *What did you like about them?*

Continuing with the whole group:

1. *What surprised you?*
2. *What difference did the statements make?*
3. *How do you see using this in the future?*

Translation to the work setting:

- Use to review a past situation or possible scenario to work through possible ways of managing it from a strengths-based perspective versus problem-based
- Use one-on-one to help someone process a different way to behave or think through a situation
- Build into training on "difficult conversations" by substituting the script for people sharing an issue they'd like help with and then participants help each volunteer to figure out how to start a conversation off on the right foot

Exercise

2. Scaling – Lily pad Style

At a breakout session of a conference filled with professionals who didn't know each other, we wanted to get them thinking about the topic of recognition and realized quickly they were facing similar issues across their heterogeneous organizations. We asked everyone to come to the front of the room and explained one side of the room represented the very early stage of being an "egg" and the opposite side of the room the "frog". We asked a series of questions related to the topic of organizational and team recognition and asked them to stand near the "lily pad" that best represented where they were in their recognition culture metamorphosis (from very early days as an "egg" to fully evolved "mature frog" cultures). Everyone quickly realized where they needed to focus their attention, and it gave us a good gauge where the biggest pain points were so we could zone in on those topics for the greatest value-add for the session. We closed the session with scaling again using those same questions, this time about where they planned to be in a year after having implemented the strategies they selected.

This exercise is great because it:

- Can be used as an energizing warm up
- Gets people thinking about the topic
- Can be done with audiences that know each other well or not at all
- Is quick to explain and perform
- Can be a "bookend" for any session - the same scaling can be done at the beginning and then repeated at the end to check buy-in or readiness

Materials:

- (Optional) 7 green vinyl cut-outs in the shape of lily pads (note: you can do this without the prop if you're in a pinch, just describe the scale)

Instructions:

1. Ask everyone to stand up and go to the part of the room where you have laid out 7 "lily pads" in a line (one lily pad for each stage in a frog's metamorphosis)
2. Explain:

   "This is a scaling exercise where I am going to ask you where you are at in terms of very new or young in your evolution of a particular skill or strength, right through to 7, which represents full maturity and consistent use of a particular skill or strength. You will stand in relation, on that 1 to 7 scale, to where you feel you are at in that evolution. In other words, where are you along that continuum from egg to tadpole to mature frog?"
3. List strengths and skills, having people physically move to the lily pad that represents where they are on the continuum. Note: encourage people to notice what's going on around them during this exercise.
4. Debrief

Debriefing Questions:

- *What did you notice about where you stood in relation to other people?*
    - *What surprised you?*
    - *What was affirmed for you?*

- *What does this say about skills and strengths in your work setting?*
- *What could you do more or of differently now you know this about others' skills and strengths?*
- *How could you leverage scaling?*

Translation to a Work Setting:

- Teams can apply this to a variety of topics such as change, transitions, recognition, satisfaction, progress on a project, collaboration, etc.
- Incorporate as an energizer for a meeting, training session or retreat
- Use translate a subjective evaluation to a quantitative scale

3. Most Memorable Moment

*This exercise has been adapted from *Mark McKergow's "Sparking Moments"* exercise in the book *57 Solution Focused Activities* and has been used successfully in various workshops.

At a solution focused train-the-trainer session, Brenda had the privilege of experiencing this activity as a participant since one of the trainees - Domenica Giacomini decided to facilitate this exercise as her assignment. Brenda chose the completion of writing their book (*Forever Recognize Others' Greatness:* Solution Focused *Strategies for Satisfied Staff, High Performing Teams and Healthy Bottom Lines*) as her most memorable moment. After answering all the questions and hearing herself say these things aloud, she was overwhelmed with feelings of accomplishment and pride." *I don't know if I would have allowed myself these feelings had I not experienced this exercise,"* said Brenda during the debriefing.

This exercise is great because it:

- Helps people find and build on many tiny aspects of success
- Allows people to speak about an accomplishment without feeling conceited
- Encourages people to build on their success and identify possible next ideas, projects, or goals from a place of success
- Requires little preparation
- Can be used with groups that are meeting for the first time to groups that work together every day

Materials:

- Pen and paper
- (Optional) Flip chart or whiteboard

Instructions:

1. In pairs decide who is A and who is B
2. Encourage people to think about a small and yet significant moment - "a most memorable moment"

   Part one - Most Memorable Moments:

3. Person A asks person B to describe "a most memorable moment" at work during the past few weeks - when they felt best about being at work (remembering that nothing is too small to consider a memorable moment)
4. Person A then asks person B (with Person A writing responses down):
   - *How come that moment was most memorable?*
   - *What was it about that moment that made it memorable for you?*
   - *What else?* (ask several times)
5. Provide three minutes to generate as long a list as possible of the reasons that made the moment memorable
6. After three minutes change roles

   Part 2 – Spotting Talents, Passions and Virtues:

7. Once you both have lists of what made your partner's moment memorable, think about what you now know about your partner's talents, passions and virtues.

8. Provide a minute for everyone to quietly reflect and pick out two compliments they want to share with their partner based on what they just learned.

9. Share the compliments with each other: "*Based on what you just said, it seems to me that perhaps you are a ---------- person.*" (This can be written on a flip chart or board for all to see).

10. Debrief by asking how many were able to come up with the two compliments to share and how did everyone react to hearing the compliment.

Part 3-Small Steps (Building on Strengths):

11. Now that we know what made our partner's moment exceptional and have discussed two of their strengths, let's build on that to find some small steps which might increase the chance of more memorable moments in the future.

12. Again in pairs, Person A asks Person B :

    - *If these qualities were to play a more significant role in your work life, what would you notice?*
    - *What else?* (ask several times throughout)
    - *What small signs would your colleagues/supervisor/ significant other notice?*

13. Person A asks person B to suggest a couple of small goals for him or herself to take in the next few days, building on everything that was discussed. Again write down what your partner says. You have four minutes this time!

14. After eight minutes total, ask people to switch partners and papers. Begin steps again with roles reversed.

Debriefing Questions:

- *What was useful about this exercise?*
- *What was interesting?*
- *What surprised people about how it all worked?*
- *What have you learned about yourself and others?*

Translation to the work setting:

- Use in a team meeting when you need to infuse some energy, when the meeting is not going well, or when a new team member starts
- Incorporate as a fun orientation exercise where people get to know each other from their most resourceful place
- At the beginning of a project, use as a way to remind people of memorable moments of previous work done well to intentionally carry it forward into the current project

Exercise

4. Solution Focused Conversations - FROG Style

At the beginning of a training session with a new group, individuals formed pairs to interview each other using these cards. People had positive conversations and learned things about each other that they would not have otherwise known. Although some of the questions participants found unusual and initially difficult to answer, by the end individuals felt empowered, optimistic and positive about themselves and each other. One participant said, *"I learned so much about my partner I didn't know yet! We've worked together for years yet never had this type of conversation before! We've committed to having these types of conversations more often, when we have lunch together, are stuck on a project, or even suggest them to our manager for the start of team meetings."* Sometimes when we're learning something new we're so afraid that we're going to ask the wrong question at the wrong time. This exercise shows you when you're always asking other people solution focused questions, it doesn't matter when you ask people what question, you can ask any resourceful questions randomly and it will help!

This exercise is great because it:

- Gives people a voice
- Demonstrates the value of powerful questions over trying to solve others' problems
- Allows exploration of issue from many perspectives
- Is a great icebreaker for energizer
- Helps people get "unstuck" from rigid mindsets or behaviours that frustrate them

- Demonstrates how to easily work solution focused questions into conversations where normally problem-based dialogue would take place

Materials:

- FROG Cards (available from www.greatnessmagnified.com or www.bzmsolutions.com)

Instructions:

1. Explain what the FROGS acronym stands in the deck of cards (which you can keep straight as they are colour coded):

    F - future oriented

    R - relationship focused

    O - opportunity seeking

    G - greatness goals

    S - scaling solutions

2. Create pairs (you can decide if you wish them to dig deeper into relationships by having them partner with someone they work closely with or learn new things about someone they don't know well).
3. In pairs, ask them to decide who is Person A and who is Person B
4. Ask all to think of a personal or work related issue they need clarity on and would like to work through
5. Provide each person with a card of each of the 5 colours
6. Person A asks Person B all questions, without first explaining the context or issue at hand, until all the questions have

been asked and answered (note: order of cards does not matter here)

7. Person A provides 3 genuine compliments related to what they've heard
8. Reverse and repeat steps 6 and 7 so Person B asks the questions of Person B

Debriefing Questions:

1. *What did you learn from your partner that was surprising or insightful?*
2. *What did you experience in the art of asking meaningful questions?*
3. *On a scale from 10 to 1 with 10 being the most resourceful someone could be and 1 being the opposite of that, where were you at the beginning of this conversation? Where are you now?*
4. *Did the questions have an impact?*
5. *Did the order of them make a difference?*
6. *What question(s) worked best for you?*
7. *What do you know about yourself as a result?*

Translation to the work setting:

- Begin team meetings, training sessions or any other organized group experience in a positive light by using randomly or specifically selected FROGS card questions as the focus for a brief conversation
- Distribute one card to each team member at the beginning of a meeting or session. Task everyone to ask their question

of as many colleagues (even clients and partners) as possible before the next gathering where insights will be debriefed

- Select a card and use it to ask it of people across the organization at different levels in order to understand when individuals are at their best and see patterns of when the group collectively will be functioning optimally

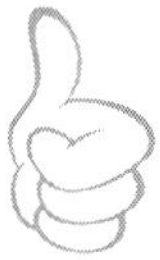

Tip! Check out www.f-r-o-g.ca for a sample of questions or to be directed to where to purchase the deck of cards

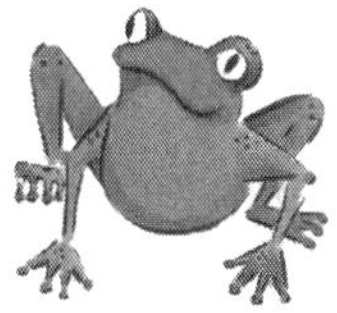

CHAPTER 2

Finding Greatness Everywhere: The Ten Dimensions of Greatness

"Never underestimate the power of dreams and the influence of the human spirit. We are all the same in this notion: The potential for greatness lives within each of us."
—Wilma Rudolph

The exercises in this chapter help to make the concept of greatness concrete. We define greatness as "living our true potential by leveraging our talents, passions and virtues"; these exercises enable you to tap into the greatness within yourself and others in a variety of ways to fit any work context. Our best hope is to prepare you so you are ready to explore how the 10 dimensions of greatness show up within yourself, your closest peers, and the broader team. Let's jump in!

Exercise

1. Metaphor: Greatness is Like...

In writing workshops, this exercise is often used to get authors' creative juices flowing; why not use it for groups? Recently at a public workshop, filled with people who had never met before, participants were asked to look around the room and list off all the things they saw or thought of. A long list was captured on the flipchart, and then everyone was asked to pick an object and use it to finish the sentence, *"[My object] is like my greatness in that it…."* We were in awe of the powerful statements everyone came up with! Participants were asked to select the one statement that resonated most and write it in bold letters on an index card to post in a location they would see every day. At the end of the session, they read their card beginning with *"I am…"* (e.g., *"I AM…genuine caring for others; "I AM…the ethical compass of my family and organization"*). As one participant said after she shared her statement, *"I have chills! I am this person, and yet I've never been bold enough to say it out loud. Oh, that's another one! I AM bold! Watch out world!"*

This exercise is great because it:

- Unlocks creativity by activating the right side of the brain
- Takes little time to explain and execute
- Is energizing
- Is something anyone can lead – It doesn't take an expert facilitator
- Can be done individually, in pairs or as a group

Materials:

- Flipchart, whiteboard, Smartboard or other surface to record ideas visible to the group
- Flipchart or whiteboard markers

Instructions:

1. Generate as many random words as possible in a few minutes
2. In your groups, pick one word from this list
3. Using that word, individually create 5 to 7 statements that follow this formula:

   " *(your topic/focus)* *is like* *(object)* *in that...*"

4. Then, combine those words into a big list, and start creating ideas from that list. It could be metaphorical or literal translations
5. Once you have this big list, identify the one that is right for you (see next exercise)

Debriefing Questions:

- *Of all the thoughts generated, which one gives you the most energy? What are you most drawn to?*
- *What is it about this idea that has the most meaning for you?*
- *If we invited you to "live" this, what might it look like?*
- *What will the end look like? Where are we heading in this journey?*
- *What need or want will it fulfill in me?*

- *What even deeper need underneath the one you noted above, will it fulfill? Is there another need below that?* [repeat until at the root of what is needed most]
- *What deeper need will this fulfill around me? What connection does this have to others or the environment I'm living/working in?*
- *What might the first next step be?*
- *How do I want to celebrate when I have taken that first next step?*

Translation to the work setting:

- Use anytime you need some "right brain" thinking. If logic or black and white thinking is stifling creativity and innovation, step back for a moment to get creative with this exercise
- If practicing as a group, ask for a left-handed and right-handed volunteer to stand on either side of the whiteboard, Smartboard or flipchart to record words as fast as possible (allows the person facilitating to stay focused on the participants and keeps things moving quickly)
- You can do this with a team. Everyone brainstorms and either through discussion (to gain consensus) or voting, narrow down the most meaning idea collectively. Then use the same debriefing questions using "we" instead of "you"

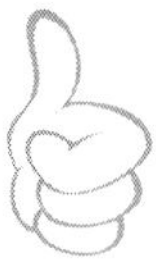

Tip! Check out www.f-r-o-g.ca for a video on how this is done.

Exercise

2. FROG Strengths

This exercise was first introduced to Brenda when she returned to an organization to follow up with some of the team members about how they were implementing the solution focused approach into their culture. A talented Child and Youth Worker introduced the FROG template with a list of positive adjectives, inviting people to circle their strengths. This led to a lively discussion which included numerous ways to adapt the exercise.

This exercise is great because it:

- Is a self-reflection on your strengths
- Can be further resource croaking (enabling others can recognize you)
- Can be done in pairs or smaller groups
- Propels you towards your goals

Materials:

- Large frog template (downloadable FROG template or pick your own from Google Images)
- Thin markers

Instructions:

1. Select a frog template and print to fit a large sheet of paper
2. (optional) If people have not been introduced to FROG - "Forever Recognize Others' Greatness" - explain the acronym

3. List on the template all the things you do in a day that give you energy and make you feel at your best
4. Underline the things that you would like to spend more time doing
5. Around the edge of the FROG write down additional things you know give you energy and make you feel your best. You may include things that you may have forgotten and stopped doing
6. Pair up with someone who you know the best and share your completed templates
7. See if you have other things to add to each other's templates
8. Determine if there's something on the inside of the template that you want to bring forward

Debriefing Questions:

- *What did you discover? What insights did you have?*
- *What is your energy level now compared to when we started?*
- *What is it like focusing on your strengths?*
- *What did you identify as giving you energy that you are committed to continuing or doing more of?*

Translation to the work setting:

- This exercise can be done in team meetings, through peer supervision, or during one to one consultations
- Print off a large frog (need a high resolution image) on a poster or banner sized paper and make it a team exercise

- Utilize this exercise with groups that are feeling fatigued or unmotivated
- Bolster leaders' resiliency by incorporating into training or a retreat

Tip! Download the frog template from www.f-r-o-g.ca or pick an image of a lily pad or frog from Google Images with a wide central space for writing in. There are lots available!

Exercise

3. Fortune Cookie

Brenda often ends facilitated sessions with this exercise. Often people in the room remark: *"I needed to receive this message right now. It is amazing how you pick the message specifically meant for you in the exact moment you needed the reminder."* Our brains are hardwired to make connections, including creative, positive ones, so why not give them the opportunity?!

This exercise is great because it:

- Allows you to relate to the concept of greatness in a creative way
- Provides an opportunity to reflect on your own
- Is adaptable to different settings
- Is fun - who doesn't love opening a fortune cookie?

Materials:

- Fortune cookies (can buy in bulk food stores or packaged in some grocery stores)

Instructions:

1. On your own or in a group, take one fortune cookie. Read it aloud
2. On your own, reflect on how this message connects with your greatness. If in a group setting, others should comment on what immediately comes to their mind when they hear that message and think about your greatness

3. People may choose to share their message and its meaning aloud
4. Record the reflections so you can see them at a later time. Don't forget to place the fortune cookie message (with the date on it) somewhere you can refer to when you need a boost!

Debriefing and Reflection Questions:

- *How does your message connect to your specific talents, passions, and virtues?*
- *What came to mind that surprised you?*
- *What were you reminded of?*
- *What might you want to do more of?*
- *What might you want to do next?*

Translation to the work setting:

- Start off a team meeting this way. Use the fortune cookie messages as a way to think about the team's greatness instead of individuals' greatness
- One person takes a fortune cookie and without initially sharing names, talk about someone in the group that embodies that and why (you can decide whether or not to then give the message to the person - it could be just as powerful not to!)
- Enjoy as a treat at orientation. Consider how the messages does or does not fit what you know already about the organization and its people. Get to know others and what they know about the organization you are all joining.

Exercise

4. What Is Your "ing"?

This exercise was initially inspired at the end of a solution focused conference where a group of trainers were meeting to discuss the highlights of their past year, share resources, exercises and create new ideas. Someone shared their daughter's business card which was populated with all the adjectives that best described her work. Brenda was inspired to use this exercise the very next week at the end of a compassion fatigue workshop with a group of health care workers. She was glad she did; as she was packing up, one of the nurses shared with her that she had something in her pocket. It was a piece of paper that she explained had her hourly wage recorded. Whenever she wondered why she came to work, she would look at the paper as a reminder. Brenda was surprised when she proceeded to rip the paper. She remarked: *"I don't need this any longer. I will now put my "ing" card in my scrubs pocket and whenever I need a reminder of why I come to work, I will pull this card and read it."*

This exercise is great because it:

- Can be done quickly
- Can be done one-on-one and in small to large groups
- Allows people to self-reflect on their strengths
- Requires little planning or set-up

Materials:

- Small blank business cards (or individuals can be asked in advance to bring their own business cards in if they have one)

- Pens or fine tipped markers
- Paper

Instructions:

1. Ensure everyone has a business card (their own or blank). If using a blank card, on the one side, write down your identifying information (e.g., name, business title, number). To save time, people could tape their business card to that side at the time or upon returning to their office.
2. Next, reflect on what really matters to you and who you really are as a leader or employee. Ask probing questions such as:
    - *What are you known for?*
    - *How would people describe you?*
    - *What makes you unique?*
    - *What value do you bring to the workplace and your organization?*
    - *What is most important to you?*
3. Once you have reflected, you can write on the blank side of the card all the things that define you with each word needing to end in "ing" (e.g., caring, organizing, mentoring, planning, supporting). You will likely come up with a combination of things you do as well as what you stand for
4. Next, underline the 5 "ings" that best describe you and how you want to be known. Discuss how this business card is now an acknowledgment of both the roles you occupy in the organization as well as the gifts you bring to the role

Debriefing Questions:

- What are your most important "ings" and why?
- How do you live your "ings" in your current job?
- What, if any, "ings" are dormant or less pronounced than you would like? What is the impact of this?
- If you could live more fully into all 5 "ings," what might you do differently?

Translation to the work setting:

- Start a project with this exercise encouraging everyone to share their special talents in the form of "ings"
- Use this exercise as a team building experience, having everyone share their "ings" with one another
- Create a team list of "ings" as a description and reminder of what is most important to the team

Exercise

5. Greatness Everywhere

The following exercise is an adaptation of a homework assignment Brenda learned from Steve DeShazer. Steve would ask family members at the end of a therapy session to imagine that a miracle had happened and everyone was behaving as if this was so. Without telling anyone, they were to choose one day to behave differently and see greatness all around them. All family members were to guess which day their loved ones were behaving differently and notice all the nice things people were doing for one another. This set up positive paranoia! The exercise below creates the same phenomenon. Once we look for greatness within ourselves and others, we notice it all around us.

This exercise is great because it:

- Demonstrates what you focus on grows
- Enables increased "noticing" of greatness already present
- Is inexpensive
- Is energizing

Materials:

- Notebook or a journaling App

Instructions:

1. Select one day or one week and notice all the great things that are happening for yourself and others
2. Write down every observation you make or comment you hear
3. Specifically notice the ripple effect when greatness shows up (e.g., impact on attitude, emotion, productivity, etc.)
4. At the end of the day or week, review the list

Debriefing/Reflection Questions:

- *What greatness did you notice in yourself?*
- *What greatness did you notice all around you (colleagues, clients, etc.)?*
- *What difference did it make when you noticed greatness?*
- *What did you notice were the benefits of noticing your own and others' talents, passions, and virtues? (e.g., effect on emotions, thoughts, attention, productivity, attitude, etc.?)*
- *What was different from when you started this exercise to when you finished it?*
- *How might you continue in a way that feels fluid and genuine?*

Translation to the work setting:

- At a staff meeting, agree to observe greatness, perhaps assigning a different day per person (can be double or tripled up depending on the size of the team and duration of time chosen). Read out a few key observations at the next staff meeting of the greatness already present

- At a staff meeting, use the debriefing questions
- Assign a secret observer to each person and have them pay close attention to that person during the week, complimenting them, and secretly doing small things for them. See if people can guess who their 'secret observer' was
- During a training session or retreat, scope the exercise where people are asked to concentrate on this for 20 minutes and debrief when people were in positive paranoia!

Exercise

6. Give 'em a FROG

It amazes both of us how a tiny squishy FROG can bring such meaning to a conversation or moment. There are times when participants were handed a frog and actually kissed it. Others collect them and have a display in their offices. Some pay it forward to others and most go to the local dollar stores to purchase their own collection in order to spread the "frogging" farther.

This exercise is great because it:

- Is inexpensive
- Is easy to do
- Creates a ripple effect that can create mindset and culture shifts
- Bridges FROG between our personal and professional spheres

Materials:

- Small frog paraphernalia (e.g., squishy frog, plastic figure, stickers, cards)

Instructions:

1. Keep your preferred frog paraphernalia handy at all times (e.g., in a purse, pocket, backpack)
2. When you see someone's talents, passions or virtues on display, pull out a frog and hand it to the person

3. Explain: *"I want to FROG you; FROG standing for Forever Recognize Others' Greatness - and the greatness I notice in you is...."*

4. If they shirk off the compliment, reply with affirmation of its importance. *"I appreciate humility is a virtue. I also really want you to hear me when I say..."*

Debriefing/Reflection Questions:

- *What is it like appreciating someone in the moment?*
- *How does this impact the likelihood of you repeating this behaviour?*
- *How can this affect the culture of your organization?*
- *What ideas do you have about how to keep the FROG factor going?*

Translation to the work setting:

- People could be encouraged to "pay it forward" by giving the frog to someone else when they notice greatness in others
- In a group setting or meeting, hand out a frog to each person. Ask them to give their frog to the person sitting beside them with the reason they deserve it. They could also give it to someone in the room they want to recognize, and then that person gives their frog to someone else until everyone has received a frog and been told why they deserve it
- Start a team meeting with a "FROG moment", where people talk about the difference being FROGed (with or without the actual object) meant to them that week

- An adaptation is writing down acknowledgments such as on kudos cards -great if the written word is preferred or frog paraphernalia is hard to come by

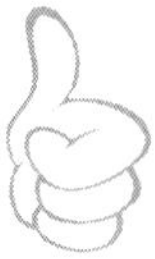

Tip! You can use small business sized FROG kudos cards (or order from www.greatnessmagnified.com)

Exercise

7. Exploring Current and Future Strengths

*This exercise is reprinted with permission from the creator *Shelley Halls*, a talented staff member at *The York Centre* (Richmond Hill, Ontario)

Brenda first experienced this original exercise when she was facilitating a train-the-trainer session. Each participant was asked to take a portion of the solution focused model and come prepared to train the group on that subject. Shelley arrived with this exercise. Imagine Brenda's delight when she realized how Shelley had taken the concept of FROG and tied it directly to the pivotal solution focused concept of complimenting. Not only is it important to learn how to genuinely pay a compliment, it is as important to learn how to accept them and internalize them as part of your own unique greatness. This wonderful exercise accomplishes both.

This exercise is great because it:

- Reminds you that we all have many strengths
- Encourages you to gain perspective, dig deeper, and prove your worth to yourself
- Motivates you to build from within and identifying others' strengths to build upon

Materials:

- Green and Blue markers
- FROG Template (downloadable or create your own from Google Images)
- Lily Pad Template (create your own from Google Images)
- List of positive adjectives (downloadable

Instructions:

1. Distribute a template full of a variety of positive adjectives
2. Take a moment and think about the strengths you already have
3. Use the green marker to highlight or circle the strengths you feel you already have
4. Use the blue marker to highlight or circle the strengths you plan to work on
5. Use the lily pad to fill in any other strengths that may not be listed that apply to you
6. In a group, each participant can share three strengths they are most proud of and one strength they would like to work on with steps for how they are going to build on it

Debriefing Questions:

1. *What did you discover about yourself?*
2. *When you dug deeper, what strengths did you realize you had?*
3. *Now that you are aware of them, when asked about your strengths in the future, will you remember to include them?*

Translation to the work setting:

- Use in supervision or coaching sessions to help clients dig deep for strengths
- Facilitate as a team building exercise, focusing on the strengths people contribute to the team

- Use as a leadership team to explore each others' strengths

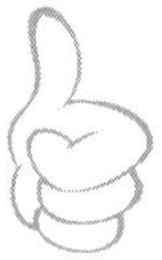

TIP! Download template from www.f-r-o-g.ca or create your own by searching hundreds of options on Google Images

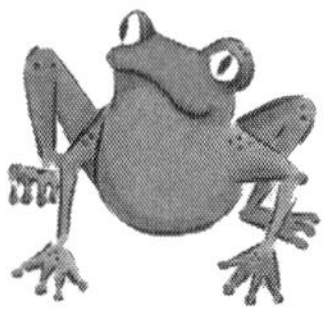

CHAPTER 3

Start With Yourself: How to Free Your Inner FROG

"To be yourself in a world that is constantly trying to make you something else is the greatest accomplishment."
—Ralph Waldo Emerson

When we practice self-recognition consistently and value it, it not only grounds us in our own greatness, but it awakens us to the greatness already present all around us. We have provided a host of tools that can be used to deepen your self-recognition practice. Our best hope is for you to take these strategies seriously and practice them; the more you make self-recognition part of your everyday reality, the more resilient and resourceful you will be in work and for the most important people in your life.

Exercise

1. Protecting Time for Greatness

*This exercise comes from *Kim Shepherd* of *Decision Toolbox* in her book "*The Bite Me School of Management*"

Decision Toolbox (DT) staff and leaders use this approach any time they need to concentrate on a single task to make progress (i.e., every day!) In fact, every new employee is given an egg timer as a symbol of the importance of balancing productivity with wellness; all are encouraged to set the timer for 40 minutes to work productively flat out and then take 20 minutes to recharge. They have found that committing 40 minutes of focused time throughout the day yields much greater productivity and a shortened work day than unplanned and unfocused long days.

This exercise is great because it:

- Makes you more productive and focused
- Increases your sense of control and satisfaction in work accomplished
- Helps get through busy days and long "to-do" lists
- Easy to teach and understand
- Can be brought to small to large sized groups

Materials:

- Timer (e.g., egg timer, Smartphone)
- Pen/paper, journal, journaling app or computer with Microsoft Word

Instructions:

1. Mute phone, put a sign "do not disturb" on your door and make all attempts to eliminate distractions
2. Select the most important thing to focus on (e.g., set your business priorities, write a blog post or section of your book, plan a conversation with a co-worker, build a budget)
3. Set your timing device so that it counts down from 40 minutes and set it to alert you when time is up
4. Start timer. Work uninterrupted for the set time (really discipline yourself not to let any interruptions that aren't how you define urgent take your focus).
5. At the sound of the alert, record your last thoughts then let it go for 10 to 20 minutes. Discipline yourself to repeat the process

Debriefing Questions:

- *On a scale of 10 to 1, with 10 being extremely and 1 being the opposite:*
    - *How productive would you say you are now after completing the exercise?*
    - *Where are you normally on a given day?*
    - *How accomplished do you feel?*
    - *How energized are you?*
- *If you were one step higher on any of the above scales, how might you adapt this exercise so you were even more productive and fulfilled in your accomplishments?*
- *How could you apply this approach to other aspects of your work and personal life?*

Translation to the work setting:

- Select a reflection from our book *"Forever Recognize Others' Greatness: Solution Focused Strategies for Satisfied Staff, High Performing Teams and Healthy Bottom Lines"* as your focus for your uninterrupted time
- Identify a problem or topic that your team continues to "circle the drain" on. Agree and set time aside to come up with as many possible solutions and opportunities to it. Pick one at the end of that time (through consensus) and try it
- Set aside time at a team meeting to discuss all the team's accomplishments and successes
- Schedule time in your calendar at least once every day for this exercise. If you can't protect that time (and we'd challenge you that you have more control over your calendar than you think you do), then reschedule that time for yourself just like you would if you had to bump someone else

Exercise

2. The Free-Writing FROG

To get us focused and motivated to write our book, *"Forever Recognize Others' Greatness: Solution Focused Strategies for Satisfied Staff, High Performing Teams and Healthy Bottom Lines"*, we each disciplined ourselves to do this exercise. We wrote all the experiences, ideas, and benefits we had to offer in the book, as if we had already written it. Wow, what a motivator! All of a sudden we didn't think how much was in front of us, we just focused on all the benefits and joy we would have in sharing this with others.

This exercise is great because it:

- Allows you to use your own unique "voice"
- Can be done as a solitary reflection or incorporate discussion that facilitates opportunities for acknowledgment by others
- Can be done with small to large sized groups
- Is suitable for all age levels
- Creates understanding about the intention behind our direction

Materials:

- Pen/paper, journal, or journaling app

Instructions:

1. Find a quiet place free of distractions and ask others to not interrupt you for a set period of time

2. Using your preferred writing medium, write about your talents, passions and virtues. Do not over think, correct or even worry about grammar (yes, we're suggesting no punctuation is needed and certainly no spell-check!) If you are struggling to free-write about your greatness, try one of the following strategies:

    a. Put yourself in a specific moment in time where you were at your best and recall every detail as if you were reliving it

    b. Write as if someone were speaking about you as if you were not present (we call this "resource gossiping") because writing in the third person can free you from the shackles of being humble

    c. Propel yourself into the future, imagining you are already successful in your desired future, and tell the story of how you were able to achieve what you did

4. Read over what you wrote. Underline the most important parts. Everyone has a different way of noticing what is important (e.g., if you're kinaesthetic, you may have a bodily sensation such as a feeling of lightness or warmth)

5. Look at everything you have underlined. Look for the themes and see the bigger "story" of your greatness and when you are at your best

Debriefing Questions:

- *What is the story of your greatness?*
- *How can you FROG yourself on a regular basis when your talents, passions, and virtues show up?*

- *How did this feel? If you initially felt challenged, how did you overcome it?*
- *How do you feel now that you have completed this exercise?*

Translation to the work setting:

- This is a great coaching exercise. If someone is feeling disconnected from their greatness and stuck, you could suggest some focused time to reflect inwards in this way or you could record them speaking it out loud (which is especially great for extraverts). Use the debriefing questions to reflect on their greatness with them and their effectiveness
- Individuals struggling to see each other's' greatness can do this exercise, instead of about themselves, but about the other person. When they underline key aspects, it could be the things they most rely on and value in the other person
- This is a great end-of-year or New Year focusing tool. What has worked last year and what will you carry forward into the New Year for professional and personal success and growth?

Exercise

3. Greatness Wheel

*This is often taught in coaching training and has been adapted for in this workbook

At a women's retreat, where the focus was on finding balance, participants were asked to identify the most important elements of a "great life". After completing the exercise below, one participant shared, *"Wow, I had no idea how much I had been putting others' needs before my own. I thought I was pretty balanced, but I realize now that's because others kept saying I was. I know why I keep getting colds and sometimes snap at my family. I need to take care of myself, which allows me to show up whole and happy. It's actually unselfish to spend time doing what I need to nurture my greatness."* You can bet she quickly moved into action to address this imbalance!

This exercise is great because it:

- Provides structure to be able to reflect in a holistic way about your life
- Is easily modifiable for different topics and foci
- Can be used one-on-one to large groups
- Is relatively easy to explain
- Is quick to complete

Materials:

- Wheel handout (downloadable)
- Pens or fine tipped markers (3 different colours)

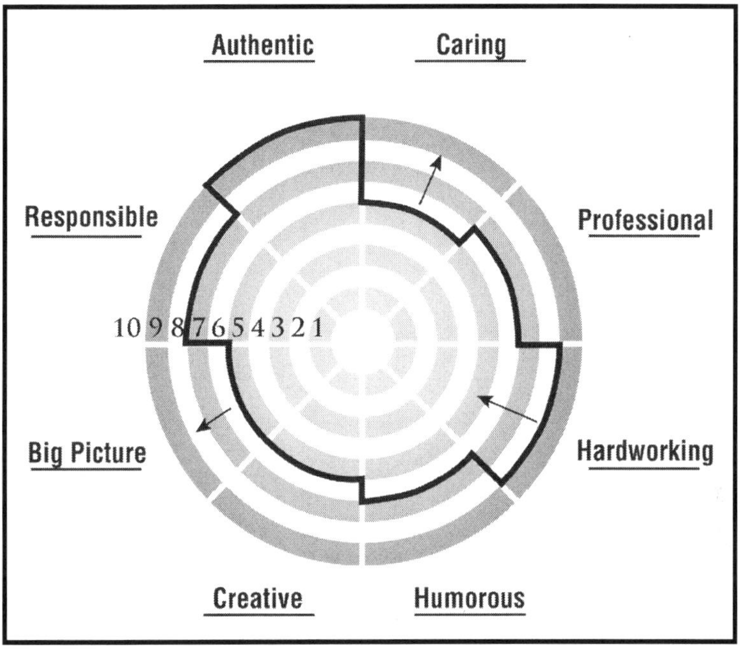

Example

Instructions:

1. Think of a time when you were at your best.
2. For 10 minutes uninterrupted, free-write everything you think of; include specific details of your thoughts, feelings, and surroundings during that very specific point in time when you were living into your greatness. Do not correct, over think, or change anything. Your paper may look messy and the words more rambling than you would ever write if someone were reading it!
3. When you are done, go back and read over what you wrote. Highlight anything that gives you energy when you read it (some people experience a physical sensation

of lightness, warmth, gut reaction, etc.; it's an intuitive process).

4. Read over the words and phrases you highlighted. Consider what you feel about this list; note what are the most important factors in your greatness
5. Record these elements of greatness on each "slice" of your Wheel
6. Consider each slice of the wheel on the scale of 10, "I am consistently and fully living that element of greatness" to 1, which is the opposite of that. Mark this using a solid line within each slice of your wheel (i.e., if one slice of your wheel is "Honesty" and you feel only sometimes in some aspects of your life you're being fully honest, you may put a solid line in that space at the "5" mark). Evaluate this three times (using three different colours):
    a. *Where are you right now?*
    b. *Where would you be if you were living your most fulfilled life? Note: not all have to be a 10 as not all may be equally essential to you – there may be "higher order" aspects of your greatness*
    c. *Where do you want to be in three months from now?*
4. Reflect on this (use debriefing questions below).

Debriefing Questions:

- *What seems to be in balance between your current life and your ideal?*
- *What "slice" of the wheel deserves particular attention and focus? What would the result be?*

- *What "slice" has already been a source of focus and work, and what has been the result of that? Of these lessons, what could be used in another "slice?"*
- *How has this exercise confirmed or brought insight into why you might be feeling a certain way (general mood or about certain people/situations)?*

Translation to the work setting:

- Have your team map out the 8 most important elements of a high functioning team. Follow the steps and then discuss where individuals feel the team is at in the current, ideal, and future state. Discuss where there are differences in opinion. Identify the most important "slice" to focus on and brainstorm options. Identify the one next step including what success will look like
- Translate your recent team engagement or satisfaction survey to the wheel. Map out what the results are saying in terms of high engagement/satisfaction areas to low. Decide as a team what "slice" could be the focus (e.g., easiest to improve upon, quick win, most important). Brainstorm strategies and implement one step at a time
- Use as a new team to establish norms. Identify 8 key aspects of a high performing team and where they want to be in 3, 6, and 12 months. Use this to create an action plan to achieve it, and reflect on indicators of success at each of those milestones. Individuals collectively or anonymously could complete the wheel at each point to populate the ratings

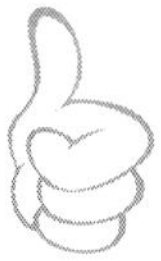

Tip! Check out the downloadable tool at www.f-r-o-g.ca

Exercise

4. Complimenting Exercise

*This exercise was created by *Dr. Heather Fiske* and reprinted with permission

At the end of a training session with postgraduate students, one participant shared with Brenda a very powerful story. The best compliment she had received was from a client who said, "*You are the best therapist I have ever had. You are so down-to-earth, you really listen, and you have made a huge difference in my life.*" What the client didn't know was that this therapist had just returned from maternity leave and was feeling torn. She didn't think she was making a difference and wondered whether she should quit. This compliment helped her decide to continue working and set a renewed path for her career. Twenty years later she was still working at the same organization having a positive impact on many.

This exercise is great because it:

- Encourages you to reflect on when you are at your best
- Reminds you of what is important to you so you can stay true to it
- Can be done in small to large sized groups
- Can take as little as 10 minutes and as much as 30
- Increases the likelihood of repeating what is working versus becoming distracted by what is not

Instructions:

1. Have the questions below written on a PowerPoint slide or on a flip chart

2. Move In partners. One person asks the following questions while the other answers:
    - What was the best compliment you ever received?
    - What made it great?
    - What made it believable?
    - When would it be helpful to remember that compliment again?
3. Reverse roles and repeat the questions above.

Debriefing Questions:

- *What did you learn?*
- *What surprised you?*
- *How could you remember the compliments in the future when you are not feeling particularly resourceful?*
- *How is it helpful to remember these compliments?*

Translation to the work setting:

- In a coaching or supervision setting, follow this formula and debriefing questions
- Use as a prep to "resource gossiping" exercise in a meeting or training session to enable people to learn about each other at their best
- Leaders can get to know their staff - new or existing - by asking about and sharing best compliment. Listening to understand what matters most to the individual enables the leader to understand where she or he will thrive, be most productive and engaged

Exercise

4. Mirror Mirror

*This exercise was created by *Gary Minden, Brenda's* husband.

When Brenda's husband Gary notices that Brenda is having a challenging day or doubting herself, he approaches her and says, *"It's time for mirror mirror."* He holds up his hand (his mirror) in front of her, looks into her eyes and says, *"Repeat after me..... I am beautiful and I am loved!"* She responds, *"I am beautiful and I am loved!"* The mantra always leads to the same result. She tears up, smiles, and feels grateful for his thoughtfulness. Almost instantly she refocuses and moves on with a better frame of mind.

This exercise is great because it:

- Takes only a few minutes
- Requires no prep or materials
- Reminds you to acknowledge how worthy you are
- Leverages repetition to allow the true meaning of the acknowledgement to be absorbed

Materials:

- None!

Instructions:

1. Identify the statements that you need to hear repeatedly and formulate it into a brief mantra

2. Give a close colleague, family member or friend permission to intrude when necessary, placing their hand in front of you as a your mirror
3. They state the mantra looking into your eyes with your full attention
4. You repeat the mantra back
5. Repeat as often as necessary!

Debriefing Questions:

- *What did you learn by doing this exercise?*
- *What surprised you the most?*
- *How is it helpful to remember these statements?*
- *How can you begin to incorporate these statements for yourself?*

Translation to the work setting:

- In a coaching or supervision session, encourage the person to create their own mantra for times of need
- If you notice a friend, colleague or close family member struggling, offer to brainstorm what they need to feel more confident about and help to formulate it into a mantra. Get permission and encourage them to give permission to others to practice this mantra when they seem to need it
- Use as a reflective exercise In a meeting or training session to enable people to learn about their challenges and allow them to create another voice that will inspire them during challenging times

- If a team is struggling, create a mantra together of what members need to be able to say to each other when it's a tough day or someone is struggling. Maybe a few mantras will be necessary! And don't hesitate to keep changing them as needed

Exercise

6. Creating a FROG Pond

Brenda had the privilege of observing one of the Child Youth Workers at The York Centre (Richmond Hill, Ontario) at the end of a school day. She was overwhelmed with pride as she experienced the power of FROG in action. The Child Youth Worker was doing a rose ceremony where he was asking everyone in the class to identify the best part of their day (the rose), the most challenging part (the thorn) and the thing they most looked forward to the next day (the bud). A young woman who had her bag packed and was ready to go wanted no part of this. Instead, she chose to leave the class. A few minutes later she returned with a huge smile on her face, a bounce in her step and a story to share. *"I just got another frog!"* she declared as she held up this purple squishy frog for all to see. Not knowing exactly who I was or why I was there in the classroom that day, I asked her if she knew what FROG stood for. She looked at me as if I was daft and said: *"Of course! It means Forever Recognize Others' Greatness."* I asked what she had been recognized for. She replied shyly, *"I help with the younger kids and the other teachers wanted me to know they appreciate it."* Then off she went to her locker in the classroom. She stopped and turned to me with another smile on her face and said, *"By the way, I have a pond in my locker."* She held up a group of multi-coloured frogs. I smiled back at her. She had no idea how she had made my day! And, how she would inspire this exercise!

This exercise is great because it:

- Reinforces the power of FROG
- Serves as a reminder of your greatness
- Can be scaled to small to large sized groups
- Helps keep the FROG and recognition momentum going!

Materials:

- Paper and pen, journal or Journaling app
- Collection of frogs and other paraphernalia

Instructions:

1. Throughout your day, whenever you are recognized, thanked or complimented on anything you do, create a one or two word reminder for yourselves
2. Perhaps like the young woman above, you may receive an actual frog. Keep track of the reason you received the frog
3. In a place you call your own, a locker, a journal, or a sock drawer if you like, place all your reminders. These are your lily pads of life - your frog pond!
4. If you feel the need to be reminded of the value you offer others, visit your frog pond and relish in your recognition-worthy attributes!

Debriefing Questions:

- *What is it like reviewing the compliments you received over time?*
- *How is it helpful to remember these compliments now?*
- *Imagining that your pond will be growing over time, what strengths will still be recognized and which new ones will appear?*

Translation to the work setting:

- At a workshop, training or staff retreat, encourage people to notice and recognize each other throughout the day by writing messages and putting them in a special spot in the room designated the frog pond. Read them out at the end of the day
- Buy a special frame, bulletin board or other wall hanging that allows you to stick or clip notes. Make recognition visually appealing in your personal space by posting it somewhere special!
- Capture at least one thing you want to recognize about yourself or someone said about you that day on a piece of paper and post-it at the end of every day (or during if you catch yourself thinking it!) Commit to creating your "pond" of recognition full by doing this every day for at least 21 days (until you form a new habit!)

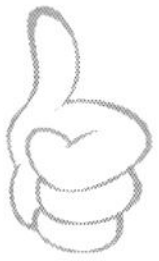

Tip! Check out www.greatnessmagnified.com for blog posts about other versions of self and team recognition rituals.

Exercise

7. Retirement Day!

A coaching client of Sarah's (who gave permission to share her story) was struggling to decide which of three possible career paths to take. Sarah assigned her this homework: Envision yourself at your retirement party. Visualize it in great detail - what does the room look like, how is it decorated (if at all), what food is served, who is present, etc. Next, write your retirement speech as if you were in that moment. At the beginning of the next coaching session, Sarah's client said, *"I know which path I am going to take! It became so clear once I looked back on my career. Only one of my three options will allow me to say what was most important to me by retirement!"* After months of feeling uncertain, she was crystal clear and a month later, working in a job on that path!

This exercise is great because it:

- Can be one privately, one-on-one or in pairs
- Is forward looking therefore helps get people "unstuck"
- Relatively easy to explain and execute
- Helps individuals get to know each other and what they most value at work quickly

Materials:

- Paper or journal
- Pen or pencil
- Noisemaker
- (Optional) Retirement signs, posters, napkins
- (Optional) "Happy Retirement" cake

Instructions:

1. Explain that the purpose is for everyone to think into the future and put themselves into the headspace of their retirement day (you can make this fun...who doesn't like to think of retirement?!) Encourage participants to think as if was their actual retirement day in the present tense

2. Have everyone close their eyes. Walk them through this visualization:

   You have just walked into your retirement celebration. Look around. What do you see? What sort of space is it? How, if at all, is it decorated? Is it large or small? Is it fancy or low key? In the office or off-site? Is it busy or intimate? Who specifically are present and what parts of your life have them come from - work, family, friends, former colleagues, former classmates? What is the mood? How are you feeling? What are you thinking?

3. Form pairs. Person A shares their retirement speech with Person B (for up to three minutes). Person B takes notes (as close to what is actually said as possible)

4. Give the signal that time is up after five minutes. Person B shares up to five words to describe the type of career Person A had had. Person A simply replies *"thank-you"* recording them on their sheet if she or he feels they fit

5. Switch. Repeat steps 3 and 4 so Person B can share his or her retirement speech

6. Individually, participants review what is written, underlining the most important words or phrases. In other words, if their career didn't include these elements, it would be unfulfilling and inauthentic. A pattern should emerge of *the* most important elements

Debriefing Questions:

- *What are your talents, passions and virtues that are most important to contribute in your career?*
- *How is your current circumstance a good fit? How could it be a better fit? What influence could you use to help make that happen?*
- *What talents, passions and virtues will you require from others to complement yours?*
- *What do you need from a team to contribute your best? From an organization?*

Translation to a work setting:

- Use one-on-one in coaching to explore with individuals their ideal role and get clear on next steps
- Incorporate into talent development and performance review conversations. This is a great way to explore how to best support your high potentials and ensure you are offering them opportunities that align to who they are (versus organization assuming what is best for them)
- Use as a team to better understand each other's talents, passions and virtues. Makes it fun! Make "you're retired" invitations, bring in retirement balloons and napkins, and have a cake that says "Happy Retirement!" Take turns giving retirement speeches. Not only will you learn a lot about each other, you will laugh together too!

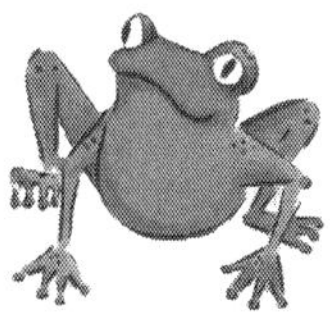

CHAPTER 4

Enable Greatness for Healthy Team Ecosystems

"A good team, like a good show, comes into being when the separate individuals working together create, in essence, another separate higher entity - the team - the show - which is better than any of those individuals can ever be on their own."
—Gary David Goldberg

In our book we talk about a team that went from being the least satisfied and engaged team to the most improved in employee engagement scores in the history of the organization, and in fact, of any organization the engagement survey company had ever studied! It took hard work and focus. We are thrilled to provide you with some of the tools that the team used to move the engagement needle. Greatness is available for any team. It's a matter of focus, persistence, and belief. Our best hope is for you to experiment and try different ways to ignite the flame. As it builds, recognize those that join in!

Exercise

1. Give 'em a Pat on the Back

An organization had just been through a huge restructuring, and the remaining leaders came together at a kick-off retreat. It had been a distracting few months, reapplying for their former or different jobs and waiting to hear if they "made it." Everyone naturally had gotten pretty introspective, distracted by their own behaviour and thoughts. It was time, with the knowledge they had a job and a clear view to who their team would be, to focus outward. One of the first exercises of the day required everyone to pin a piece of cardstock on their back and together say *"I have your back"*. Then, they went around and wrote on each other's cardstock what they knew they could rely on in him or her or what was most admired. When the exercise was finished, each unpinned the paper and read the multitude of reasons why they were valued and how they knew they could support their colleagues. Years later, you could see the cardstock taped on the walls of the leaders' credenzas. It was a pivotal reminder "it's a new day" and "we're all in this together because we are all needed".

This exercise is great because it:

- Can be anonymous or people can make the feedback personal
- Allows everyone in the group to receive feedback
- Can be done quickly
- Can be done in small to large groups
- Is energizing - physically and psychologically!

Materials:

- Safety pins
- Cardstock
- Fine tipped markers (preferred but pens or pencils will do)

Instructions:

1. Take your safety pin and a piece of cardstock. Find someone in the room who can pin the cardstock to your back.
2. Taking your marker, pen or pencil with you, walk around the room, writing what you would like to acknowledge about each person. It may be something you have told them before, or maybe something you would like to recognize as a strength or skill you have never shared
3. Continue until time is up or you have given feedback to everyone
4. Unpin the cardstock and read the comments
5. Reflect on what you notice about what your colleagues recognize as your strengths, gifts and talents

Debriefing Questions:

- *What surprised you about what your colleagues shared?*
- *What talent, passions and virtues are most valued by your colleagues? How can you contribute even more of this?*
- *What was the experience of providing feedback to colleagues like? How can you find other ways to keep sharing what you value in them?*
- *What would you like to do with this information? What's next?*

Translation to the work setting:

- Have people post their feedback cards in their work stations or somewhere they will see it regularly
- Have a "wall of awesome" where everyone can have their feedback posted together in the work environment
- Incorporate the feedback into formal performance appraisals
- Practice as a team, having people's cards posted to the wall for people to record during the week and review at a future meeting or celebration

2. Give this Gift to Someone Who...

*This exercise was written by *Dr Heather Fiske* and *Brenda Zalter-Minden* taken from the book: "*Education and Training in Solution Focused Brief Therapy*"

In our book "*Forever Recognize Others' Greatness: Solution Focused Strategies in Satisfied Staff, High Performing Teams and Healthy Bottom Lines*" we told you about the most improved team, and how their very first step toward building a better future happened during recognition week at work. They said they wanted to do something as a team for about fifteen minutes during work hours. Brenda bought a box of chocolates and wrapped it in many layers of paper, putting a compliment on each layer – for example, "*Give this gift to someone who smiled at you today,*" or "*Give this gift to someone you trust.*" When Brenda returned for the first fifteen-minute meeting, she presented the gift and the instructions. Each team member was to pass the gift to a member who fit the compliment they uncovered. This continued until everyone had received a special message. The bonus was they shared the chocolates, some laughs, and hope. Some still have the message they had been given. It is also not out of the ordinary for team members to use "gift" language, telling their colleagues what a difference they made for them that day or why they value them.

This exercise is great because it:

- Is a fun way to celebrate together
- Low expense but high perceived reward
- Can be adapted to the situation and time available
- Enables a depth of interaction with a small to medium sized group in a short period of time
- Makes people feel good without singling out individuals (as everyone in the group receives acknowledgment)

Materials:

- Statements (downloadable)
- Box of chocolates or other treat(s) the team could share together
- Wrapping paper or newspaper
- Tape

Instructions:

1. Purchase a gift the team could share together (e.g., a nice box of chocolates or truffles).
2. Download or create your own statements to help individuals to recognize their colleagues then print them off
3. Place a statement on the gift then wrap it (note: we suggest starting with *"Give this gift to someone generous"* so they share the gift at the end of the exercise with their colleagues!)
4. Place the next statement on the wrapping paper and wrap it. Continue until all statements are wrapped (ensure there is one statement minimum for the number of people you expect to be present at the meeting)
5. At the meeting, provide people the following instructions:
    a. Please take the gift and pass it to a person who meets the criteria on the statement
    b. This person then keeps the compliment and will unwrap the next layer, reading aloud the next statement and passing it to a person who meets that criteria
    c. Keep this process going until all statements have been read and given out
    d. Ensure everyone receives at least one compliment

5. Enjoy the gift together when finally unwrapped!
6. Encourage everyone to keep their statement to remember the acknowledgment they received from their colleagues

Debriefing Questions:

- *What did you appreciate about this exercise?*
- *What did you learn about yourself that you may not have known before?*
- *What was reinforced for you?*
- *How can you use the acknowledgement at another time?*
- *How can you ensure you remember this at an important time?*

Translation to the work setting:

- As written, this can be part of any meeting, workshop, or gathering
- Use it at a retirement party or gathering with a guest of honour. The statements could be used to spark acknowledgments about the guest of honour. Everyone takes a turn to unwrap the gift, reading the compliment, and then sharing a share a story about the guest of honour related to that compliment. When it is finally down to the last statement, the guest of honour gets to make the statement and then keep the gift
- Use this as a way of celebrating a milestone. Consider statements that are about what the team is most proud of in their achievements. It can be a great morale booster and re-connecter when people are feeling disjointed, transitioning, and overloaded.

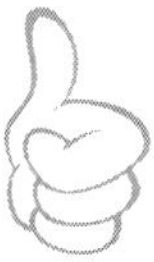

Tip! Check out the downloadable tool at www.f-r-o-g.ca

Exercise

3. Resource Croaking (Gossiping) – Exercise 1

**Brenda* first experienced and learned resource gossiping as an exercise from *Peter Szabo* in one of his excellent workshops.

The first day back from break, teachers at a private school came together for a whole day of teambuilding and individual goal setting. Two new teachers were introduced to the group. Mid-afternoon Sarah asked the teachers to get into groups of four to "resource gossip" about the things they believe to be true or know to be true about each other phrased in a way of what they appreciate, admire or rely on in the people present. The trick was they had to talk about each person individually as if they weren't there. In other words, she told the teachers to gossip (imagine!) but in a healthy way. During the debrief, the teachers said they felt uplifted that their colleagues believed in them, remembered their gifts when they hadn't been together in months, and were energized to start the year with an appreciation for each other. Perhaps most touching was when one of the new teachers, who had been very quiet all day, shared, "*I feel so fortunate to work with such an observant, kind-hearted, and passionate group of women who share the same love for children and teaching that I do. I had no idea you could know me so quickly, and I thank you for that. Before today I was nervous but now I know you have already decided I will be a success!*" Wow. Don't you just want to grab three friends or colleagues right now and try this exercise?

This exercise is great because it:

- Is energizing
- Can be done in small to large groups
- Can take as little as 15 and up to 45 minutes for a deeper dive

- Builds positive energy
- Can be used with groups have just known each other for a few hours to years

Materials:

- Cardstock or paper
- Pens
- Any device to track the time
- Noisemaker (especially if you have large group)

Instructions:

1. Explain the concept of resource gossiping (see pages 47 or 59 of our book *"Forever Recognize Others' Greatness: Solution Focused Strategies for Satisfaction Staff, High Performing Healthy & Healthy Bottom Lines"* or search Sarah's blog at www.greatnessmagnified.com). If you've really embedded FROG into your team or organization, you can call it "Resource Croaking"!

2. Have people form groups of 3 or 4 (no more than 4 and try to have people for the same sized groups so they are finished at the same time). Ask them to determine who is Person A, Person B, and so on.

3. Explain the exercise, and remind them you will cue them when it is the next person's turn. Reinforce it's important to not shirk off any compliments, and each person should end their turn with two simple words, "thank-you".

4. This next step can be done standing up or sitting down. Person A turns his or her back to the group. The others then "resource gossip" about Person A for the next 2-5 minutes

(set the time depending on how much you have and be sure to tell them when time is up). If the group is at all struggling, you could share these questions as starting points for the discussion (it should feel fluid and natural though, not like a question and answer!):

- *What strengths, talents, and gifts does this person have?*
- *What lesson, observation, or story can you recall that exemplifies this?*
- *What do you value in the person?*
- *Where do you believe the person will be successful?*
- *What impression do people get right away about him or her?*

5. At the end of the allotted time (usually 1 minute), signal (with a noisemaker is necessary) it is time to switch

6. Person A turns to the group and simply says "thank-you"

7. Steps 4 to 6 are repeated for Person B and the rest until all have had a chance to resource gossip and be resource gossiped about

Debriefing Questions:

- *What was it like to be on the receiving end of "resource gossip"?*
- *Were you aware of all the things your colleagues said about you?*
- *How could you use this outside of this session? How might this be applicable to other settings?*
- *How does it impact your thinking about gossip?*

Translation to the work setting:

- Explain the concept of resource gossiping to others. Make it a familiar concept. Point out it happens fluidly anyone someone shares something positive about someone else when they're not around. Acknowledge how great it was to be a part of resource gossiping
- Resource gossip as much as you can! Maybe set a goal to say something positive about someone when they are not present every day for the next 21 days until it becomes a new habit
- Notice when you're tempted to gossip. See if you can turn it into resource gossiping. Can you see the strengths and gifts rather than only the negatives?
- Resource gossip across teams! At an organization-wide retreat, follow the same steps, but when someone turns their back, people resource gossip about that person's team. Make sure to write down everything that people say about your team and bring it back to your team!

Exercise

4. Resource Croaking (Gossiping) - Exercise 2

When Brenda first utilized this exercise with an intact working team at the beginning of a workshop, it was very clear how frightened people became. There were rolled eyes, moans and groans. Participants had nice things to say about one another but were visibly concerned that nobody would have anything nice to say about them. They were actually worried people would write negative things on their sheets. Once the morning portion was complete, it took a very brave soul to stand up and read the compliments out loud. Once all the people had their turn, there was a huge sigh of relief. Some were actually moved to tears! Others were overwhelmed with what people wrote and made comments such as: *"I worked here for 17 years and never knew people felt this way about me"* and *"I guess people really get me."*

This exercise is great because it:

- Allows people to begin to identify greatness with less anxiety (writing is easier for some than speaking about greatness)
- Is great for introverts
- Supports recognition among team members even if they are strained (i.e., everyone has some strength they can find which gets acknowledged in this exercise)
- Enhances team morale
- Is structured
- Allows the facilitator to see where the strengths are in individuals and in the team as a whole

Materials:

- Cardstock or paper
- Pens, pencils or fine tipped markers

Instructions:

1. Write "*What I value most about* _______" at the top of the paper and add your name on the line.
2. Pass your paper to the right. People record what they value about each person
3. Once everyone has had a chance to write on everyone's paper, return it to the person who is named at the top
4. Ideally, people read it out loud by changing the language so it's personalized: "*I am valued for my* _______"

Debriefing

- *What was your energy like when this was first explained to you? How is it now?*
- *What was the experience like of giving and receiving feedback in this way? What worked?*
- *What happened when you had to stand up and personalize the list?*
- *How could you adapt this into your everyday work or meetings?*
- *How can you continue to utilize your teammates' individual strengths?*
- *How will you intentionally bring the strengths recognized by others as valued assets to the group?*

Translation to the work setting:

- Facilitate this exercise at the start of a new project to remind people of the value they bring
- Use in team meetings and post around the room as a way to remember and appreciate the diversity of individuals' greatness
- Use in supervision or coaching sessions
- Make it FROG themed. Print the downloadable FROG from www.F-R-O-G.com or search Google Images for a frog that has a lot of whitespace to provide room to write. Print it on cardstock and use this instead of blank paper

Exercise

5. Who Says That?

Even sitting around the pool in sunny Boca Raton, Florida can be exhilarating when you talk to your friends about your new book idea and they share an exercise they created to do with their team. Brenda would like to thank Natalie Leuchter for being an inspiration in many ways and for this fun exercise!

This exercise is great because it:

- Is simple
- Generates camaraderie and connection within a group
- Encourages laughter and light heartedness
- Is unique and fun

Materials:

- Ongoing list of team members' common, unique, and fun expressions

Instructions

1. A leader and/or team member listens for unique and fun expressions each team member may use and repeat frequently, recording them
2. The expressions are kept and saved for another time. You can decide how long you want to save them
3. When ready, at the beginning of a team meeting ask: "*Who says this?*" State an expression and allow all to guess
4. Keep going until you run out of expressions

Debriefing Questions:

- *What did you like about this exercise?*
- *What have you learned about your coworkers?*
- *How is humour helpful to you and the team?*
- *When would it be helpful to do something like this again?*

Translation to the Work Setting:

- This can be done with any team at any time. Build it into a team meeting or social event!
- Try this exercise at the beginning of a long training program as an icebreaker
- Start recording expressions at the beginning of a project and then do this exercise as a way to celebrate at the project's end

Exercise

6. Complain, Complain, Complain

*This exercise is an adaptation of *Moan, Moan, Moan* written by *Rayya Ghul* in the book: *"Education and Training in Solution Focused Brief Therapy"*

Although we often teach this exercise for frontline service providers, it was actually a group of middle managers that really stands out in our minds as gaining the most from it. They were feeling fatigued in having a "revolving door of complaints." When probed further, we quickly learned that they were "firefighters," solving problems and taking on crises. We wanted to help them deepen the listening to what people really needed, which often resides *behind* the complaint. Leaders quickly found that when they took the role of Complainer, they ran out of steam within 2½ minutes, and the listener realized just how fast they normally jump in (*"I found I had to stop myself from interjecting. It felt I was listening for such a long time, not under 3 minutes!"*) Leaders collectively realized that they were expending more energy than they needed to, when in fact what their staff wanted most of all was to be heard and seen as having something important to say. One participant's smart grandfather shared a metaphor with her that we now love to pass along to anyone who experiences this exercise. *"Every conversation is a potential fire. In one hand you have a pail of water and in the other you have a pail of oil. It is always your choice what you choose to put on the fire."* Genuine heartfelt compliments are water to any situation.

This exercise is great because it:

- Reinforces active listening in a realm (negativity/complaining) that most people agree they would like to experience less of
- Can shift negative energy to positive (in a training session/meeting or an individual's perspective in general)

- Is relatively quick to explain and run through
- Requires no demo
- Can be added "in the moment" as there are no materials or prep required
- Provides hope for people exhausted with negativity

Materials:

- None!

Instructions:

1. Ask all to get into pairs, picking a Person A and Person B.
2. Person A is the "listener" and will not interrupt Person B, rather only listens for 3 things to acknowledge about their partner
3. Person B identifies an issue that is unresolved in their personal or professional life they are prepared to talk about for 2 ½ minutes
4. When the facilitator cues to start, Person B speaks about the issue uninterrupted for 2 ½ minutes
5. At the 2 ½ minute mark, Person A shares 3 genuine compliments
6. Switch and repeat steps 4 and 5

Debrief:

- *What were you thinking or feeling about your issue before it was your turn to share during the exercise? How was it similar or different after?*

- *What happened to the energy and dialogue after you acknowledged the greatness (seeing past the negativity)? What happened as a result?*

- *How might you handle customers, staff, colleagues, or others differently with this strategy? How might it get different results than you have been getting now?*

- *How do you see this related to the topic of recognition?*

- *Who or what group could you try this with and what do you expect will be the result?*

Translation to the Workplace:

- Use in customer service training

- Incorporate into one-on-one coaching at a point when someone is stuck in negativity, fixating on what is not working

- Use in performance appraisals, mediations, and other experiences where individuals can be nervous. They can benefit from an approach of interrupted listening for 2 ½ minutes by being able to blow off steam and save face.

- Practice this yourself by venting out frustrations, then acknowledge what you need or want that is missing and consider how you can these needs met.

- Help people to calm down when they come into your office all fired up! It's another version of the stress management strategy "count to 10 before speaking" by providing people with a verbal outlet to vent and wind themselves down before acting. When the rant is over or it's winding down, acknowledge greatness you are hearing so that by the time they leave your office, they are more resilient than when they came in!

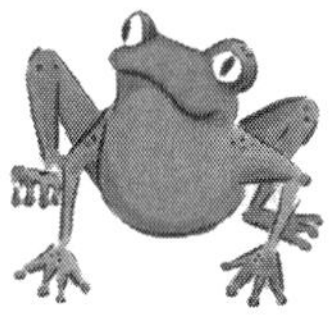

CHAPTER 5

Think FROG on a Big Scale: How to Optimize Organizational Recognition

"Recognition is not a scarce resource.
You can't use it up or run out of it."
—Susan M. Heathfield

Don't just take our word for it that FROG builds strong recognition cultures. Let's look to our clients for evidence. In 2014, a children's services agency, *The York Centre* (Richmond Hill, Ontario), made a commitment to train all their staff in a solution focused approach to support best client care and healthy workplace interactions. The frontline workers instantly latched onto the concept of recognition, specifically FROG. They created a checklist to help stay solution focused in their practice along with a recognition card that encouraged them to notice when their team members fulfilled this shared goal. They created a few central boards where the forms were available and staff would fill out the paper and post on the board for all the team members to see. One of the most impactful results was the surprise of reading the board and seeing their own act of greatness acknowledged by a colleague. It encouraged those not initially completing the tool to begin doing so as the ripple effect of acknowledgment was evident in more smiles, laughter, effective therapeutic interactions, and new team collaborations. Our best hope is for you to read these exercises, try some and discover the greatness within your places of work.

Exercise

1. SOAR Analysis

*This exercise was adapted from *David Shaked's* work in his book "*Lean Six Sigma: A Strengths Based Approach*" based on the creation of *SOAR* by *Jacqueline Stavros,* for more information on *SOAR* refer to "*Thin Book of SOAR: Building Strengths-Based Strategy*"

This exercise was facilitated during leadership training as an alternative way of preparing for their annual strategic planning process. The conversation was lively and everyone was positive, future focused and complimentary. People were happy to experience that they all were on the same page and had very similar ideas and goals. By the end of the session, there were clear goals for next steps and many priorities had already been established. A side benefit was that they wanted to make sure they had a list of all the questions so they can begin to ask them of their managers, supervisors and front-line.

This exercise is great because it:

- Is an effective solution focused substitute to the well know SWOT analysis
- Allows for a broad view
- Is an uplifting and motivating processing tool
- Is easy to use
- Can be used with internal and external stakeholders
- Is scalable from small to large sized groups
- Requires little preparation in advance

Materials:

- List of SOAR questions (find sample questions and see how one organization used here: http://www.uoguelph.ca/vpacademic/avpa/outcomes/SOAR.php)
- (Optional) Instructions printed or on a PowerPoint Slide
- 4 colours of Post-It notes
- Writing materials
- Flipchart or flat surface

Instructions:

1. Explain what SOAR stands for - Strengths, Opportunities, Aspirations, Results. Clarify any questions about SOAR
2. Distribute pads of 4 colours of Post-Its to participants
3. Distribute a list of questions (or project on a slide) the questions under "S" for "Strengths". Starting with the "S," individuals, dyads or small groups note one strength per Post-It
4. All Post-Its are collected and put onto a flipchart or wall that is visible to all
5. Repeat steps 3-5 for the remaining 3 letters.
6. Divide participants into 4 groups with each group taking one letter, putting the Post-Its into themes, labelling on a Post-It with a solid line around it (to differentiate it)
7. Have each group creatively present the themes back to the group (note: feel free to get creative here by having that presentation be through a poem, song, role play, etc.)

Debriefing Questions:

- *What surprised you?*
- *What was affirmed for you?*
- *Based on what you have discovered is already working, how could you ensure this continues?*
- *What is your most important next step?*
- *How could you use SOAR in other ways?*

Translation to the work setting:

- Can be used as a "go and see" for leaders to ask powerful questions in employees' work environments
- Can be put into a virtual tool (e.g., Survey Monkey) to collect feedback in advance, large amounts of feedback and/or from stakeholders who are unable to participate in the session
- Can structure a world café (learn more about the world café approach by a quick Google search or by reading the classic "*The World Café*" book by Brown & Isaacs) or other facilitated conversation formats using SOAR

TIP: To download SOAR questions, please visit http://www.soar-strategy.com/

Exercise

2. Recognition Gram

The organization we describe in this section took on recognition grams with a vengeance. Each team created their own recognition board where the grams were posted, however the uniqueness of the team was honoured by calling the gram a name that resonated for that team. One calls it "Noticing" another "Peer Recognition" (see pictures on this and the next page). They decided the best way to share the grams was by publicly displaying them on boards throughout the organization. Momentum built and this board is never empty or houses "stale" grams.

This exercise is great because it:

- Builds exponential energy through the power of "surprise" recognition
- Is fun and engaging
- Is customizable to culture and creativity
- Keeps the positive energy going after or between retreats, training and meetings
- Can be completed virtual, person-to-person or as a group

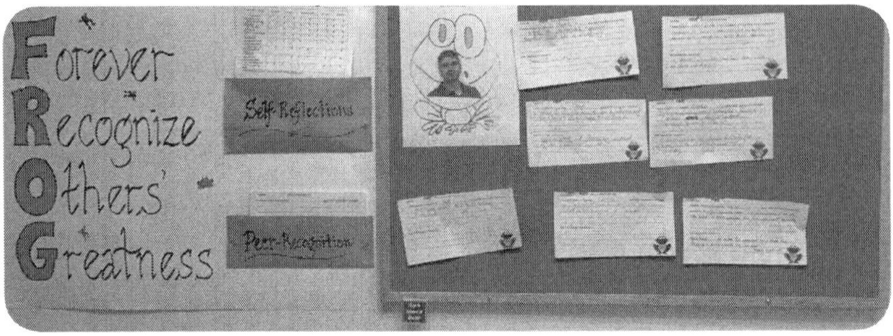

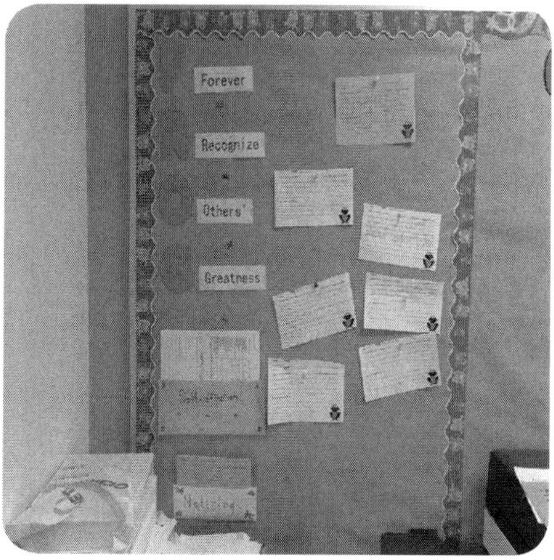

Materials:

- Recognition cards (create your own or purchase from www.greatnessmagnified.com/store)

Instructions:

1. Make the recognition cards available in the workplace or by handing them out
2. Share the purpose: write a recognition gram for a colleague any time you see something worthy of recognition
3. Distribute the grams in the way that best fits your work environment or tradition (e.g., hand delivery, submit to a central place to be later read aloud or distributed at a team meeting, post in a central location such as on a bulletin board, etc.)
4. Optional: This may be more work, however, may be useful to mark a key milestone, wherefore grams could be submitted to a central person or department, and then on one day they get distributed organization-wide to all the recipients of a gram

Debriefing Questions:

- *What difference did you notice once you instituted recognition grams?*
- *How do these grams affect the culture of teams and the organization?*
- *Where did teams maximize the opportunity from using grams and where might some teams still yearn for more recognition? What can be done to carry forward the best of one team's results to bolster the efforts of another?*
- *What would be a valuable next step? How can you build in new approaches? How can you raise the energy and commitment level?*

Translation to the work setting:

- Use it at a team or organizational social (e.g., quality of work life barbeque). Hand out 3 to 5 as people arrive and have them fill out the cards before they leave (that the organizers can deliver later) or distribute them that day to the people that deserve their recognition
- Virtual workplaces or large organizations may prefer technological platforms to automate recognition grams
- Use stickers, toys (e.g., little squishy frogs), cards, buttons or other fun things where people write a word or two of recognition
- The idea can be used for a fundraiser by having people purchase a gram for a small amount or donation, using that money for a charity of choice or in the case of a not-for-profit organization, your Foundation

Exercise

3. Recognition Checklist

*This exercise was inspired by the checklist in *Stubblefield's "The Baptist Health Care Journey to Excellence: Creating a Culture That WOWs!"*

Every time Sarah starts with a new team or gains a new team member, she hands out a Recognition Checklist to all her staff. One new staff member was having a down day and Sarah got a sense she would benefit from a lift. Sarah looked up on the Checklist how she liked her tea or coffee, then went and bought her favourite tea (green with ½ a sweetener). When she brought it to her, she said, *"I just wanted you to know that I have been hearing great things about you already from your clients and I am glad you have joined the team."* The recognition was important. Saying it in exactly the way this new employee liked it best (private words of praise) at a time she needed it with the surprise of her favourite tea from her new boss communicated a strong message that she was genuinely wanted and needed. Bad day be gone!

This exercise is great because it:

- Helps new leaders understand their staff and what motivates their top talent
- Is a good way to recognize individuals in a meaningful and customized manner
- Is inexpensive, low time commitment, and easy to do
- Can be done virtually or in person

Materials:

- Recognition Checklist (downloadable or create your own)

Instructions:

1. Leaders introduce the concept of a Recognition Checklist in whatever medium best fits (e.g., an email, one-on-one, at a team meeting)
2. Recognition Checklist is emailed or handed out
3. Employees complete the form and submit it virtually or in paper form to the leader
4. Ideally, the leader would have a brief conversation with each team member about how they value being recognized; if the span of control of leaders is large, this could be done as a group sharing the most common ways people say they like to be recognized
5. Starting immediately, using the strategies staff most identify with when any opportunity arises to acknowledge (making it as specific to each individual as possible)
6. Check-in at a team meeting or one-on-one how staff feel the recognition is going (use debriefing questions below)

Debriefing Questions:

- *Do you feel recognized in a way that is meaningful?*
- *Is the feedback being utilized? What more could be done? When does it already work well?*
- *Do we want to make our preferences transparent, such that the results become apparent to everyone and not just the leader?*

Translation to the work setting:

- Create a matrix of the top two ways every team member prefers to be recognized; with agreement, you can distribute, upload or post it in a common location (so all can recognize in the ways their colleagues prefer to be recognized)
- The top ways people want to be recognized could be incorporated into team meetings (e.g., if most prefer public words of praise, start team meetings with a greatness acknowledgement)
- Next celebration, pull out the preferences of what people like on their pizza, in their coffee/tea, and make sure you have all the options/varieties available (how much fun would it be to have a "sundae bar" of toppings to put on your plain cheese pizza?)

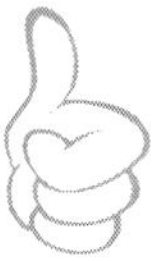

Tip! Check out the downloadable tool at www.f-r-o-g.ca

Exercise

4. Big FROG Ponds

Just as we explored in section 3 where you can create your own FROG pond, and organization turn a huge bulletin board into an organizational FROG pond. By having it at their main entrance, where *everyone* could see their shared greatness - customers, staff, leaders, donors, suppliers. Everyone was encouraged to use this as a space to write spontaneous notes of acknowledgement (kudos cards were provided), attach thank-you cards received, post posters of great things the organization was doing (e.g., food drive for charity), share positive news clippings, and attach holiday cards in December. All around the FROG Pond were awards the organization had won. The Twitter handle of the organization and a hashtag was provided, encouraging people to take a picture of the pond or share specific acknowledgement through social media. It became the central place for organizational recognition, encouraging acknowledgment at on a broader scale than ever before.

This exercise is great because it:

- Reinforces the exponential power of FROG
- Serves as a reminder of group greatness and builds shared pride
- Can be central or duplicated in multiple locations
- Helps keep the FROG and recognition momentum going!

Materials:

- Large space to create a central FROG pond (whatever format works best for the culture)

- Kudos cards, pens and materials to write notes spontaneously
- Push pins or stapler (if a bulletin board)

Instructions:

1. When you and others see something individuals or groups deserve acknowledgement for or other sources of organizational pride, record it and post it up
2. Post thank-yous, positive news stories or other acknow ledgements from external partners or customers post on board
3. Take pictures of board, selfies and write posting to share organizational pride on social media

Debriefing Questions:

- *What is it like reviewing the compliments on the board? What is the experience when you walk by it?*
- *How is it helpful to remember these acknowledgements when you're having a challenging day?*
- *Imagining that the pond will be growing over time, what strengths will still be recognized and which new ones will appear?*

Translation to the work setting:

- At a workshop, training or staff retreat, encourage people to notice and recognize each other throughout the day by writing messages and putting them on the pond. Or, read examples of what is one the board if some may have missed it

- Take group pictures in front of the board and post them! Make it meaningful by having everyone hold a sign up of what they value in their colleagues, about working there, in the organization. Or, have everyone write the name of a person or team they depend on and value. A picture's worth a thousand words!

- Capture at least one thing you want to recognize about colleagues, another team or the organization each day, writing it on a piece of paper and posting it as you leave for the day. Commit to contributing to the "pond" by doing this every day for at least 21 days (until you form a new habit!) Imagine how that could shift how you feel about your work by focusing on what is working as you leave versus the weight of what's not?

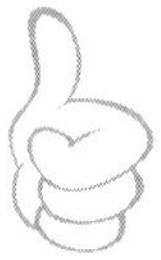

Tip! Check out www.greatnessmagnified.com for blog posts about other versions of self and team recognition rituals.

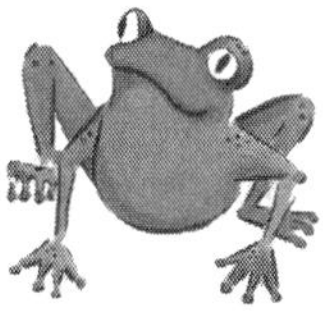

CHAPTER 6

Manage Change with Resiliency: A FROG for Every Season

"The world as we have created it is a process of our thinking. It cannot be changed without changing our thinking."
—Albert Einstein

Our best hope for this chapter is to highlight the importance of resiliency through change by offering a variety of exercises that enable you to stay healthy, strong, and positive through any transition. These tools also provide creative ways to help you understand, support, and encourage your peers, coworkers, and colleagues during challenging times.

Exercise

I. Change Resiliency Toolkit

*This exercise has been adapted by a tool created by *Dr. Heather Fiske*

A group of new healthcare managers seeking to further strengthen their emotional intelligence (EI) came to training, and left with a toolkit full of strategies to leverage their EI by remaining resilient. Even within the first few months in their new role, the signs of burnout were setting in - missing the gym, their families complaining they were home late, feeling guilty about not having enough time with their staff, etc. Sarah suggestion to build a toolkit that would keep them resilient was received with great enthusiasm. We used the metaphor of an *emergency toolkit* (thinking of all the items they would have in their car in case of emergencies) and brainstormed what the equivalent may be for their personal resiliency. They shared strategies, empathized with each other's struggles, and came up with new ideas they hadn't practiced yet. They each identified the most important next step to implement immediately to build resiliency, and another they committed to trying within a week. *"I have a newfound focus on wellness! Before I thought it was selfish to take time for myself, but now I know if I don't I won't be able to ride to waves of whatever this job brings for me and my staff!"*

This exercise is great because it:

- Provides a baseline for your current resiliency and change fatigue
- Enables reflection of what resources are already at your disposal
- Can be done individually, in pairs, or as a group
- Is scalable from small to large sized groups

- Requires no prep and can be added "on the fly" to any individual or team discussion

Materials:

- Flipchart, whiteboard, or Smartboard (in a pinch, participants can use their own paper)
- Flipchart or whiteboard markers

Instructions:

1. Draw a line down the middle of your writing surface
2. Brainstorm all the things that people have in the trunk of the car for emergencies (e.g., candle, blanket, flashlight). Record these on the left side
3. Explore what the equivalent could be for personal or team resiliency (e.g., "candle" could be "a friend that could shine a new light on the situation"). Record responses on the right side. If people have more than one idea per item, that's just fine!
4. Check-in if this seems like a good list before moving on to debriefing. If not, inquire what is missing and then check-in again.

Debriefing Questions:

- *What do you most need in your personalized change resiliency toolkit?*
- *What intention will you set for yourself to ensure you have it?*
- *What difference will this make for you or others?*

- *How can you bolster this during periods between major transitions?*

Translation to the work setting:

- If a team is struggling, they could do this together. Ask the team to commit to one thing as a group to build resiliency (only one...if they are overwhelmed finding the easiest return-on-energy strategy will be key)
- To build a sense of collaboration among a leadership team, at a meeting practice this together, encouraging individuals to share their resiliency strategies and brainstorm new ones.
- Debrief what slight changes leaders could introduce in their organizational cultures in order combat depleted staff resiliency and pick one to trial
- Create visual reminders of commitments to strategies. For example, if a strategy is "take a 10-minute stretch break every morning and afternoon), put a Post-It note on computer screens or laminate cards of a picture of what would be done on a break (e.g., a coffee mug) at work stations as visual reminders

Exercise

2. Metamorphosis Cards

This exercise has been facilitated many times for a range of groups and organizations. The end result is always the same. People thoroughly enjoy the questions and despite how stuck they may have felt initially, they always have at least one idea of where to start. They also realize through this exercise that it is the power of the questions that lead to goal setting as opposed to the person asking the questions since the rotation of chairs leads to different people asking the questions of the same person.

This exercise is great because it:

- Provides a scripted dialogue to help people navigate through change
- Offers a variety of questions so individuals can select those that sound authentic to them
- Provides an easy formula to remember
- Reinforces the heart of the FROG concept during potentially challenging conversations and situations
- Emphasizes how powerful questions can support someone working through a change, even when we know little about the change, how they feel about it or if can't empathize; it's about being present for the other person versus trying to solve, fix or assuage concerns

Materials:

- Metamorphosis cards (downloadable sample questions or purchase full set on our websites)

- Noisemaker

Instructions:

1. Divide the group in half.
2. Ask one group to form an inside of the circle facing outwards and the other half to form the outside circle, standing across from someone in the first group. This can be seated or standing however it is more energizing standing
3. Ask the people on the inside to think of a change or transition they are struggling with. Inform the outside circle participants that they are the coaches
4. Give coaches the deck of six cards
5. Inform the group that the coaches will ask all the questions on card 1 of their partner over the next five minutes.
6. Coaches ask all the questions on the card until they hear you signal time is up.
7. Coaches on the outside circle move one step to the right so they are across from a new person
8. Coaches ask their new partner the questions on the second card until they sound to cue that round is over.
9. Repeat steps 6 to 8 for the next three cards. For the last card, the Coach returns to their original partner.
10. Coaches asks their original partner the questions on card 6 which includes paying them three genuine compliments about how they have become resourceful about thinking through the change they are struggling with

Debriefing Questions:

- *Coachees, what was it like being asked questions by different coaches?*
- *Coaches, what was it like asking questions of different people without knowing the entire conversation or even the change they were struggling with?*
- *What value did you experience in* not *knowing what the issue was or full story?*
- *What questions resonated for you that you could bring back into the workplace?*
- *What questions would you like to "adopt" as your go-to questions when someone is struggling with a change?*
- *How do you feel about your role in supporting people through change after this experience? How is it similar or different from how you saw your role before we started this exercise?*
- *What are you already doing that is working in supporting people through change?*
- *Coachees, what questions would you continue to use related to this or other times when you struggle with change? How can you "self coach" using these powerful questions?*

Translation to the work setting:

- Post one powerful question from each card, noting one question per flipchart paper. Post each flipchart around a common area. Have people share their thoughts over a set period of time and reflect on the responses as a group (e.g., at a team meeting or retreat).
- Use the cards one-on-one in supervision or discussion

- Use as a project team to help formulate a resourceful project plan to get all aligned quickly
- Managers and project leads can use as a check-in at key milestones of a project or when detecting not all are on the same page (as is expected given that people transition at different paces)
- Use as an exercise to support teaching William Bridges' transitions model or other frameworks about the psychological side of change by offering a concrete tool

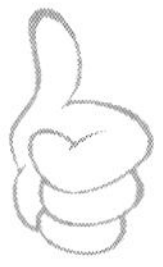

Tip! Check out our website www.f-r-o-g.ca for FROG Metamorphosis Sample Questions" or purchase the full tool at www.greatnessmagnified.com or www.bzmsolutions.com

Exercise

3. Thank-YOU Cards

During a time of massive change, Sarah and team planned a leadership retreat that focused on resiliency. Every leader was given only one piece of pre-work to do: write hand-written thank-you notes on the cards provided to any 5 (or more) of the 60+ leaders in the organization. Tell them exactly what you value in them and why. Oh, the outcry! Some said, *"This is childish! How elementary school! What if someone doesn't get a "Valentine"?"* With coaxing, all agreed to give it a try. Before long, we were asked for extra cards as 5 wasn't enough! After an afternoon filled with powerful resiliency exercises and tools, by far what leaders said was most valuable was hearing exactly how they had a positive impact on their colleagues' lives by reading it in writing. They posted the cards in their offices, shared their appreciation with the thank-you cards' authors, and kept in a place they could easily access when they needed a lift.

This exercise is great because it:

- Reinforces the importance of specific, personalized acknowledgments
- Continues the messaging of the importance of recognition especially during challenging times
- Encourages people to keep going
- Reminds people of their value and that they are not alone

Materials:

- Thank-you or blank cards with envelopes
- (optional) Stamps

Instructions:

1. Distribute cards to participants (before or during meeting, retreat, or training session)
2. Share the intention: to ensure you provide meaningful words of acknowledgment to colleagues, clients, direct reports or supervisors who you depend on, have done something worthy of recognition, to build authentic goodwill with etc. Have individuals complete their TY cards with this intention in mind. Note: you may wish to make more available so they can write as many as they like.
3. Have people put their cards in a central location, in bins/ bags with individuals' names marked on it, give directly to colleagues or mail if they are not geographically close

Debriefing Questions:

- *What did you notice about the process and experience of writing the thank-you cards?*
- *What surprised you about what was written in the thank-you cards? What was it about what you read, who wrote a card, or how you felt that surprised you most? What was the value of that surprise?*
- *How did you decide who to write cards for?*
- *How could you keep this going, as written notes or verbal recognition, in a bigger way?*
- *How could you make written recognition a habit?*

Translation to the work setting:

- Instead of cards, you could use simple kudos or FROG cards where people can write in a sentence or even just a word what you wish to recognize
- Make cards or kudos available during a meeting, training, retreat or even between sessions for individuals to spontaneously note acknowledgments when they notice someone doing or saying something deserving of acknowledgement
- For groups that are particularly "left brain," make the recognition related to something specific (e.g., project, outcomes/targets, etc.) so that it doesn't feel "touchy feely" but is clearly connected to performance

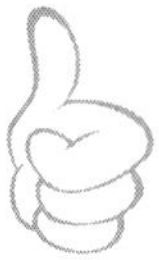

Tip! FROG thank-you and kudos cards are available through www.greatnessmagnified.com along with stories of how they have been used in additional ways to get powerful results!

Exercise

4. Transition Through Change Using Scaling in Action

This exercise was most recently facilitated during an Emerging Leaders Program in a large healthcare organization. It was an eye-opening experience for a group of supervisors when they were able to compare where they felt they were in terms of managing particular change projects compared to where they felt their teammates were. Most supervisors having had prior knowledge of the change were either in the middle "neutral" zone of the transition; they had not come to accept the change entirely yet were aware it was coming. Others were at the "new beginnings" stage of transition where they had initiated the new way. Most of their colleagues were still struggling with the impending change and were stuck in "endings". Having gained this insight was helpful to be able to return to the work environment to support their colleagues with empathy and new strategies.

This exercise is great because it:

- Brings a popular theoretical concept of "transitions" (e.g., William Bridges) during change to life
- Allows everyone to see quickly how others are adjusting
- Enables measurement of subjective feelings
- Is energizing, fun, and quick
- Can be used as an icebreaker and wrap-up activity to bookend a training session, retreat, or meeting to gauge progress
- Can be used for a group going through the same change or to help people understand where they are at in the specific change that is most relevant to them

Materials:

- None! Just need floor space to work
- (Optional) noisemaker

Instructions:

1. Briefly review William Bridges' model of transitions (or your preferred framework about the psychological side of change) emphasizing the continuum of the psychological transition through change (e.g., Endings to Neutral Zone to New Beginnings). Emphasize everyone can be at a different state in the phases of transition, and people can move fluidly by the hour/day/week!
2. Explain the scale. Indicate one side of the room represents Endings, the other side New Beginnings and middle Neutral Zone
3. Ask individuals to stand along the invisible continuum where they feel they are at in relation to the change
4. Ask individuals to discuss with those in close proximity why they chose that spot on the continuum and how they are experiencing the change
5. Call the group to attention and ask each grouping to share key points raised
6. (Optional) Repeat Scaling by asking them to stand where they think the majority of their team is (i.e., put yourself in others' shoes). Repeat steps 4 and 5.
7. Have people stand in a spot on the continuum they haven't yet stood. For Example, if you are in New Beginnings, stand in Neutral or Endings. Discuss what people at this part of

the continuum must be experiencing and what they most need. Brainstorm the best ways to provide that.

8. Call the group to attention and ask each grouping to share key points raised

Debriefing Questions:

- *What surprised you most?*
- *What did you learn? What difference does that make for you?*
- *What are you prepared to do next?*
- *If repeating this exercise in three or six months from now, what do you expect would be different and why?*

Translation to the work setting:

- Can be used any time a leader or facilitator needs to quickly gauge where the group is at on a particular issue. Can be used repeatedly to see how opinions and experience has changed over time or from specific interventions
- Can be used in strategic or program planning session to help prioritize strategic tactics according to readiness
- Can be used at a team retreat to assess quickly and transparently what people feel are the most important areas to focus on

Exercise

5. What Do You Appreciate?

*This exercise is credited to *Deri Latimer, CSP*

At a recent chapter meeting of the Canadian Association of Professional Speakers (CAPS), international speaker Deri Latimer took the group through this warm-up to demonstrate the power of using appreciation to shift brain chemistry in a healthy way. Even though most of us knew each other, it was fascinating to hear what people responded to the question *"What do you appreciate?"* It was great perspective taking for so many of us who were in a state of flux in our businesses!

This exercise is great because it:

- Is energizing, positive and fun
- Works for groups who know each other well or are meeting for the first time
- Can be done expeditiously
- Requires no prep and easy to explain
- Can be done even large groups (as long as you can get their attention!)

Materials:

- (Optional) Noisemaker

Instructions:

1. Have everyone stand up.
2. Tell participants that for the next five minutes, they are to greet as many people as possible, starting with the question, "*What do you appreciate?*" Both share and ask each other the question. Provide a different answer for every new person you meet.
3. Call the group back together.

Debriefing Questions:

- *How do you feel now compared to when the exercise first started?*
- *When you think about the changes you are experiencing right now, how does the lens of appreciation impact your experience?*
- *What stood out for you about what people appreciated? What were the themes or unique things you heard? How could those be honoured during the change even more so than they are now?*
- *How can you incorporate this exercise or a similar reflection into your workplace, particularly where change is happening?*

Translations into the work setting:

- Speak in the language of appreciation in your team meetings on a regular basis. Use it as an insulator against change fatigue.
- Recognize key people who are instrumental in supporting their colleagues and projects. Make them the focus of

the appreciation by shifting the question; *"What do you appreciate about Gloria?"* All can contribute what they appreciate about that important person.

- Focus on what is working even during transitions. *"What do you appreciate about our team?"* or *"What do you appreciate about this company?"* can help people stay grounded in why they chose to work where they did despite the situational and immediate challenges that change can bring.

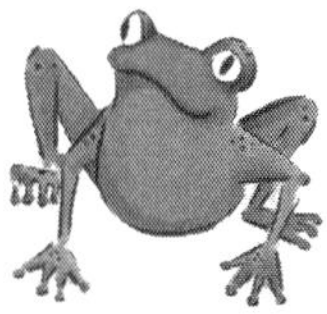

CHAPTER 7

LeapFROG Your Way through Roadblocks

"I think of them as speed bumps instead of roadblocks. Just a minor delay to get me over the hump on the highway to my dreams. You never know the things you might see if you slow down on your journey so you can learn and enjoy the moments."
—Michelle Colon-Johnson

Our best hope for this chapter is to provide you with exercises and tools to assist you in overcoming obstacles. How different would it be to view these obstacles as speed bumps on the path towards living your best life? Being prepared with handy tools ensures you will remain positive and strong. In order to support those around you, remain curious, try new approaches and tools, and go slow; one step at a time ensures you focus on how far you've come as opposed to fixating on and becoming discouraged about how far you still need to go.

Exercise

1. 4-Step Conversation Starter

*This exercise was adapted from *Michael Bungay Stanier's* work which both authors were introduced to at one of his marvellous workshops

A department with a long history of conflict decided that they needed to begin to address issues directly rather than gossiping, defensiveness, and ignoring problems. A quick tool was created to reduce the first barrier: *"How do I actually start a difficult conversation?"* Brenda introduced the tool to team members. After explaining how to use it, she encouraged them to first practice with those they felt "safe" with, then use it more and more as they gained confidence and comfort with it. As needed, she coached them, particularly in how to begin to address long-time conflicts. Quickly after the tool was introduced, individuals not only began to speak directly with each other, they also called each other on inaction; if someone was gossiping, they would reply, *"Sounds like you need to have a difficult conversation!"*

This exercise is great because it:

- Shifts the mindset that a conflict will never improve
- Gives everyone a safe way to prepare for a conflict to increase the odds a conversation will go as planned and well
- Gives everyone a common language
- Levels the playing field with those who are comfortable being assertive and those who are less so
- Challenges mindsets about conflict to see it as having the potential of being relationship-building
- Can be done with individuals who have never met to those who work closely with each other
- Can be taught one-on-one or to large groups

Materials:

- 4-Step Conversation Starter tool. (downloadable)

Instructions:

1. Provide the 4-Step Conversation Starter tool
2. Ask individuals to think of an issue they need to work through with someone or constructive conversation they would like to have with someone
3. Have individuals pair up. One person decides to go first and thinks of the issue/conversation they need to work through while their partner asks the questions on the card. When finished, the individual considers their issue and determines how they would like to proceed
4. Partner can switch so both can have a turn

Debriefing Questions:

- *How was this different from how you normally think about a potentially challenging conversation?*
- *What questions were most helpful for you?*
- *How ready were you to have the conversation before you started on a scale of 10 "completely" and 1 the opposite of that? Where are you now?*
- *What will you do differently now?*

Translation to the work setting:

- This can be done as a group if dealing with a challenging issue. The formula works with team challenges as well as one-on-one conversations
- Mediators or leaders can provide this to individuals in advance of bringing disparate parties together, particularly for individuals who are nervous or tentative about agreeing to the meeting. Providing the conversation tool as "homework" can help them think through what they most need to explore in the mediation
- Decision making around tough issues, such as budget cuts, human resource issues, etc. can be supported with this framework
- Can format the size of the tool to fit a pocket (e.g., scrubs, uniform, suit) then laminated it so everyone can keep it with them as a handy reference

> Tip! Download our version of the tool from www.f-r-o-g.ca

Exercise

2. Round Robin

The following exercise is a fun one to practice when attempting to reduce tension for difficult conversations. Brenda used it in a workshop on giving and receiving feedback. One participant shared an annoying relationship with her sister-in-law when she felt her relative would take over at dinner parties and family gatherings. She knew she needed to have a difficult conversation with her but had no idea how to start it. Once she practiced getting the conversation started, she said she now knew exactly what to say. At the next follow-up session, she reported she had the conversation and it went very well.

This exercise is great because it:

- Shifts the mindset that a conflict will never improve
- Is fun and productive
- Lessens the anxiety related to starting a difficult conversation
- Can be used personally and professionally to improve relationships
- Can be done with individuals who have never met to those who work closely with each other
- Is valuable for staff, middle managers and C-suite alike

Materials:

- Paper, journal or journaling app
- Pens and pencils

- (Optional) FROG Cards: Solution Focused Conversations deck

Instructions:

1. One person volunteers to sit at the front and share an issue that she or he are struggling with (note: in a work setting, ensure they know not use names or personal specifics)

   Round 1

2. The volunteer has 2 ½ minutes to explain the crux of the issue, focused on what is most important for everyone to know so the group can be most helpful.
3. Everyone in the room asks one clarifying question sequentially (note: note: if it's a group introduced to solution focused work, many of the clarifying questions should be solution focused such as using the *FROG™ Cards: Solution Focused Conversations*)

   Round 2

4. The volunteer turns his or her chair and gets out a piece of paper and pen to record what is discussed.
5. Everyone discussed what the volunteer is already doing well (you may recall this is "resource gossiping" which we describe on pages 47 or 59 of our book *Forever Resource Others' Greatness: Solution Focused Strategies for Satisfied Staff, High Performing Teams and Healthy Bottom Lines).* The focus is on what appears to be already working (despite the person having a problem).

   Round 3

6. Next is "wonderings". With the volunteer's back still turned, everyone gets a turn to "wonder." It's like giving advice but not directly. They can share something such as *"I wonder*

what would happen if they started the conversation by saying this...." Continue to wonder until all have shared one thing they wonder and can keep going until all the "wonderings" are out. The volunteer writes down all the wonderings that resonate with him or her. Note: back is turned so that no one feels offended that their wondering wasn't recorded and the person with the issue can focus solely on what works for them

7. The volunteer picks out the first next step via the wonderings. Specifically, the volunteer records how they might start the conversation.

   <u>Round 4</u>

8. The individual with the issue rejoins the group and identifies their next step including the first sentence they will use to start the conversation

9. The group acknowledges 3 genuine compliments of the volunteer

10. The volunteer acknowledges 3 genuine compliments of the participants who helped him or her

Debriefing Questions:

- *Volunteers, what became clear to you through this process?*
- *Participants, what did you learn or relearn about how to be most helpful for someone struggling with an issue or decision?*
- *How might you start a difficult conversation?*
- *How could this be used in the workplace? Could it be used in specific ways?*

Translation to the work setting:

- Can be used during team meetings as a case consultation
- Can be used in leadership meetings to explore collaboratively how to combat a major issue
- Can be used as a way to solicit help from a group, project team or staffing team to deal with an issue impacting them all (e.g., supplier or client issue)

Exercise

3. Compassion Satisfaction or Compassion Fatigue – Exercise I

*This exercise has been adapted from the *"paper plate exercise"* learned from compassion fatigue specialist *Francoise Mathieu*

At a leadership retreat, the continuum of compassion satisfaction to compassion fatigue (discussed starting on page 133 of our book *Forever Recognize Others' Greatness: Solution Focused Strategies for Satisfied Staff, High Performance Teams and Healthy Bottom Lines*) was introduced for the first time - a novel concept for busy leaders who didn't feel they had the right to consider how to meet their own needs. When leaders reflected on all the ways they were busy, they were surprised and realized quickly it was no wonder they were feeling so overwhelmed. For some, the reason they got into leadership was their desire to support people. Yet they had been hard on themselves feeling they were not there for those that they wanted to support. However, they could identify some ways they could get reconnected with the purpose of becoming a leader. One shared, *"all this time I thought when I didn't work I was letting my team down, but I get it now that by coming in spent every day I was doing no service to anyone let alone myself. I have to take a few things off my plate, and I know what these things are, so I can spend time doing the things that add the most value."* Before she left the session, she had spoken with her direct supervisor and peers about what she needed to stop doing or do less of with full support. Talk about getting in action!

This exercise is great because it:

- Supports caregivers and people in service
- Helps those who are not feeling resilient to become resourceful for themselves and others

- Acknowledges an individual for being a caring, compassionate person (they are not broken, but rather the irony of being extremely caring is it can leave them feeling depleted if they do not refuel)
- Provides a framework for people to better monitor their level of compassion fatigue so they are able to detect the signs of decline
- Helps to keep people resilient and satisfied (i.e., in a state of compassion satisfaction)
- Can be done with little preparation
- Builds shared empathy, understanding and trust at a deeper level
- Can be practiced one-on-on to large sized groups
- Can be done with individuals who have never met to those who work closely with each other

Materials:

- Paper
- Pen, pencil or fine-tipped marker

Instructions:

1. Draw a large circle on a piece of blank paper
2. List all of the things on the inside of the circle that keep you busy
3. Underline all the things you wish you could change (regardless if you can change it or not)

4. Circle all the things you want to change, that you can change even a little bit

5. On the outside of the circle write all the things you've lost touch with that used to give you energy (e.g., perhaps you have stopped singing, dancing, exercising)

6. Of all the things you may have lost touch with, choose one to re-introduce into your life

7. Reflecting on your circle, see what you can eliminate, even things that save a few minutes every day in order to leave room for something more meaningful you would like to add or do more of. Put brackets around them

Debriefing Questions:

- *How is your circle calling you to greatness? What greatness is already there to build on?*
- *What greatness do you wish to intentionally cultivate?*
- *What will you eliminate or do less or to make more room for what is most important?*
- *What's your first small step?*
- *Picture us together in one year's time from now. You have lived into that "miracle circle". What happened in that year to arrive there? What did you do? What are you most proud of? What resources did you leverage? What difficult choices and tasks did you have to work though? How did you know it was a good idea for you?*

Translation to the work setting:

- Teams of caregivers or service professionals can build this exercise into meetings as a check-in and agree together what to stop, start or continue doing to boost resiliency
- If feeling depleted, complete exercise and then have this conversation in supervision or with your direct supervisor
- Work with your coach to put these plans into action, removing the barriers and addressing habits that will stand in the way if left unchanged
- Encourage this dialogue in meetings and at retreats during stressful and challenging times

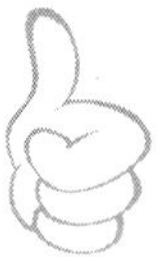

Tip! Download a Compassion Satisfaction to Compassion Fatigue Chart at www.f-r-o-g.ca or learn more in Chapter 7 of our book *Forever Recognize Others' Greatness: Solution Focused Strategies for Satisfied Staff, High Performance Teams and Healthy Bottom Lines*

Exercise

4. How Was Your Week? – Compassion Fatigue Exercise 2

Sarah used this exercise in a women's retreat full of wellness professionals. It was helpful to take the temperature of how resourceful participants were feeling. It also gave them a direction of what they each needed to focus on that would allow them to leave even more resourceful. As one participant said, *"I had no idea what was weighing me down, just that I felt like I couldn't move forward. By getting clear that I was struggling with the same things every day, I was able to focus on strategies that would counteract that heaviness. Just by doing this, I already feel lighter and I haven't even implemented them yet!"* Sometimes just a check-in can calibrate us to allow us to get into action!

This exercise is great because it:

- Enables people to figure out where they are on the spectrum of compassion satisfaction to compassion fatigue in an experiential way, making self-assessment more accurate
- Relatively quick to complete (can be done in 15 minutes or less)
- Can be practiced one-on-one and in small to large groups
- Can be done with individuals who have never met to those who work closely with each other

Materials:

- Pen or pencil
- Printout or PP slide of Compassion Fatigue to Compassion Satisfaction Chart (downloadable)

Instructions:

1. Pair up, self-selecting who is Person A and Person B

2. Person A describes things that stand out for him or her about their week for 3 minutes. The person is encouraged to really try to visualize and get back into their week. What did they do? How did they feel? What were the highs? What were the lows? How they felt physically? Emotionally? To what extent did it change much? When and what contributed to those higher versus lower periods? Retelling the experience in the present tense is important so details are given and the exercise is not a "surface" review of the week.

3. Person B listens intently to understand the experience of his or her partner's week. If necessary, in order to remember, Person B may write single words down when hearing specific physical, emotional, or behavioural words (note: can just record it on a piece of paper or circle what hear on the Compassion Satisfaction to Compassion Fatigue Chart).

4. When 3 minutes is up, Person B shares the words heard to check in if heard correctly the physical, behavioural, and psychological symptoms associated with compassion satisfaction (in the "green"), transitioning into compassion fatigue (in the "yellow") or in compassion fatigue (in the "red")?

5. Together, partners get curious about:

    a. *Where on the continuum of compassion satisfaction to compassion fatigue does Person A seem to be?*

    b. *What contributed to compassion satisfaction?*

    c. *What triggered compassion fatigue?*

4. Then, repeat steps 2-5 by switching turns
5. If you kept notes, switch papers so Person A has his or her own paper and visa versa

Debriefing Questions:

- *What surprised you about where you fell in the compassion satisfaction to fatigue scale?*
- *How can you use the "signs" or "triggers" of compassion fatigue to help you pay attention sooner to what helps you and put strategies in place?*
- *What strategies could we come up with to stay in a state of compassion satisfaction? What could help to stop the progress from yellow to red? Or to get out of compassion fatigue?*
- *How can you help people when you notice the signs they are transitioning to yellow or red?*

Translation to the work setting:

- Practice with a team showing signs of compassion fatigue. Individuals can partner up or the whole group can discuss their week as a group, with the meeting lead noting the signs and symptoms under the three headings
- Use as a coaching tool for someone needing support or a meeting about the impact of being burnt out
- In the service profession, incorporate exercise into Orientation as a proactive strategy individuals can use to monitor their own compassion fatigue

Exercise

5. Holistic Work/Life Wheel

*This is often taught in coaching training and has been adapted for in this workbook

Even the most balanced among us have areas of our life that are not as balanced as we would like them to be. Working with a group of yoga teachers, Sarah had each individual map the key elements in their lives and then rate how balanced she felt she was in each aspect of her life and where she wanted to be. Some were surprised as to which area stood out as out of balance (e.g., *"I can't believe as a yogi my physical health is out of balance. I am committing to being on my yoga mat every other day this month, and I need you all to hold me to that!"*) The group followed this reflection with the "Two Steps Forward" exercise to make commitments to improve their life balance in a key area and solicit the help from their colleagues to ensure they were successful.

This exercise is great because it:

- Can be done on your own, in pairs, or as a large group
- Is fast
- Can be done privately or shared as a group
- Is designed include what is most meaningful to you by you defining what you feel should be included in a holistic picture of your life (i.e., everyone has a unique perspective of the important elements of their life - work/career, personal, leisure, spiritual, etc)
- Can be made as "big picture" or "granular" as you need it or as required for the context this is used for
- Benefits staff, middle managers and C-suite levels alike

Materials:

- Wheel template (downloadable)
- 3 coloured pens or fine tipped markers

Instructions:

1. (Optional) Share the completed template as an example (downloadable)
2. Label the top of the paper "Holistic Work/Life Wheel" with your name and date
3. Label the spaces provided in the 8 most important elements of your life (e.g., "children," "work," "professional development," "spirituality," etc.). Each "slice" of the Holistic Work/Life Wheel should have a label when this step is complete
4. Consider each slice of the Holistic Work/Life Wheel on the scale of 10: *"I am completely satisfied with this aspect of my life"* to 1 the opposite of that. Mark this using a solid line within each slice of your Holistic Work/Life Wheel (i.e., if one slice of your Holistic Work/Life Wheel is "Leisure" and you feel only somewhat satisfied, you may put a solid line in that space at the "5" mark). Evaluate this three times (using three different colours):
    a. *Where do you stand right now?*
    b. *Where would you would be if you were living your most fulfilled life?* (Note: not all have slices have to be a 10 as not all may be equally important to you!)
    c. *Where do you want to be in three months from now?*

4. Reflect on this (use debriefing questions below)

Debriefing Questions:

To oneself, in pairs or as a whole group, debrief:

- *What seems to be in balance between current and the ideal state?*
- *What "slice" of the wheel deserves particular attention and focus?*
- *What "slice" has already been a source of focus and work, and what has been the result? Of these lessons, what could be used in another "slice?"*
- *What is the "readiness" that would facilitate closing the gap between current and desired future?*

Translation to the work setting:

- When considering a career transition, use this tool to see what aspects you love/area a good fit about your current role and what aspects are less satisfying/fulfilling. Scale how much you need to look for them in your next role and brainstorm ways you can evaluate in advance of transitioning if it will meet your needs
- When considering leaving a role, complete tool to gain perspective if the job is really "that bad" or if there might be something you can do in your current role to make it better
- As a team, label the "slices" and then consider together the areas that are working and not working. Pick only one area as a team that will be the area of focus. Brainstorm how to make it better for all then pick one strategy. Keep working on it trialing one more thing at a time to make that "slice" workable for all.

Exercise

6. Two Steps Forward

*This exercise was adapted from another exercise entitled *Footsteps by Dominik Godat* in the book *"57 Solution Focused Activities"*

This exercise was first used at the end of a series of training sessions where staff from an organization were learning how to practice using the solution focused approach. It was a fabulous way to end the training as it ensured people took responsibility for what they could implement immediately as well as what they could get started the next week. Sharing these goals with their colleagues held them all accountable for their actions. Having at least ten reasons for why people knew they could achieve this provided the boost in confidence some people required!

This exercise is great because it:

- Makes an exploratory exercise action-oriented
- Focuses on what is working - building on the strengths, healthy practices and resources already available to the person rather than considering it all an "uphill battle"
- Can be done with groups who know each other well or have only spent a few hours with each other (as long as there has been some interaction)
- Makes plans transparent to encourage accountability and peer support for being successful
- Applicable to staff, middle manager and C-suite levels alike

Materials:

- Flipchart paper

- Large and fine tipped markers (that don't bleed through – stay away from permanent)
- (optional) Painter's tape

Instructions:

1. Taking a large piece of flipchart paper, write your name in bold letters across the top
2. Draw two large feet (don't trace your own feet, make them big!) Make sure they have five toes
3. Above the left foot write "My Step Tomorrow" and above the right foot record "My Step Next Week"
4. In the centre of the left foot write your action you just came up with. On the right, record the step that will look like in a week's time from now
5. Everyone places their "feet" flipcharts around the room, on the floor or taped to the wall
6. Take your time walking around the room, visiting others' "feet" posters. Write in other's "toes" how you know they will be successful. For example, if someone wrote *"I will go to yoga tomorrow"* in the left foot, I might write a strategy in the big toe *"you can book a class before you leave today from your Smartphone"* or acknowledge an attribute such as *"you do anything you put your mind to."* In doing so, you will be supporting them to be really resourceful and act as their cheerleader in their success

Debriefing Questions:

- *Looking at your feet poster, how do you feel about your next step forward – tomorrow and next week?*

- *What surprised you about what people wrote in the "toes"?*
- *How might this approach help you gain momentum?*
- *How is this similar or different from how action planning normally happens?*

Translation to the work setting:

- At the end of a workshop or retreat where there has been a great deal of exploration, have individuals identify the concrete actions they plan to take (i.e. translate broad concepts into concrete next steps) and build in a system for checking in
- Use as a practical recognition activity where individuals can recognize teammates' strengths that they know will enable them to be successful
- Project teams can use to bring a light-hearted way to exploring next steps; can make the feet smaller on letter sized paper and then post on a wall as a visual reminder of the most important immediate and next step to advance a project forward

Exercise

7. One Small Step

*This exercise was learned from *Mark McKergow* and adapted for this workbook

At a training session with a group of managers and supervisors, the following exercise was introduced as a way to encourage people to come up with a significant and important goal as well as to remind themselves of all the things they already do well. At the conclusion of the exercise, one of the managers commented that she thought this was a fabulous way to do performance reviews with staff. It allows people to identify what they think is most important to work on first from a place of strength and resiliency. All agreed it would be a much more pleasurable and productive way to have discussions with people about their career goals and ambitions.

This is great because it:

- Encourages people to find the strengths within themselves
- Puts individuals in the driver's seat of initiating progress
- Can be a healthy and positive framework for discussing performance
- Makes big issues, concerns, or barriers to self-regard seem more manageable to address

Instructions:

1. Draw two circles (an inner circle and an outer circle) on a sheet of paper. The inner circle represents what is already working. The outer circle represents one thing you would like to get better at
2. Fill the circles using the following steps:

- Think of something that is important to you and related to the work you that you have a desire to get better at. Record this outside of both circles (in the white space surrounding the circles)
- List 10 things you are already good at (note: does not have to be work related). Record these in the inner circle. Note: if struggling, here are some prompts:
    - *What have you accomplished?*
    - *What are your talents, passions, and virtues?*
    - *What is going well?*
    - *What do others compliment you for?*
    - *What else?*

3. Consider what else you want to improve. Record these goals or best hopes in the space between the two circles. Phrase what comes to mind in positive ways (e.g., instead of "*I want to stop coming too late*" adjust to "*I want to come to work on time*")
4. Consider which goal or best hope from the outer circle could be brought into the inner circle first
5. Consider what the first small leap would be to make progress toward the goal or best hope

Debriefing:

- *When this goal or best hope is reached, how could it be celebrated or acknowledged?*
- *What surprised you?*
- *How did listing what you were good at, even if it were unrelated to the goal, have a use?*

- *What other ways could you use this or bring to teams you work with?*

Application to Workplace:

- In performance review discussions, this can help in creating SMART (specific, measurable, achievable, realistic, time-bound) goals by focusing on existing strengths while also building accountability for accomplishing current goals for improvement
- If a team has set a goal, incorporate into the setting and reviewing of that goal
- At a training session, retreat or team meeting, if the group is stuck in a hopeless or negative place about an issue or challenge, try this exercise together. See how it helps the group get "unstuck" by having them shift to a positive mindset, even briefly, before coming back to deciding the best way forward to address a situation.

CONCLUSION

We invite you to pause to celebrate your successes.

Whether you have just dabbled with a few tools or you've made a concerted effort to apply as many as possible, we want to take a moment to celebrate your greatness. You've stretched, trusted, experimented, and courageously made a difference. How do we know you have? Because we see the evidence; people who recognize (FROG) improve the lives of others around them through small gestures and by experimenting with strategies that embed recognition as a cultural norm. We are certain you are having the same success in positively contributing to your life and others'!"

We invite you to share your successes.

What worked? Which exercises lead to the most positive change? Which exercises bolstered what is already working and affirmed greatness in an individual or team? What might you do differently based on your experimentation and insights? How can you share these insights with others? Tweet with the hashtag #FROG to @greatnessmagnif and @BZMSolutions; post to our Facebook pages; write a LinkedIn blog post; join our LinkedIn Group "Recognition Pros!;" and tell all your friends and colleagues about what worked so they can try it too!

We invite you to consider what your next step is.

Have you considered, what is your next step? How can you spread FROG? How has FROG spread already, and how can this be replicated based on what worked? What other areas of your life could you bring FROG to, or upon reflection, how have you already used it? If you read our book, you will no doubt remember we concluded with the 30-Day Recognition Challenge. How have you taken on such a challenge in your personal and professional life, using tools such as these? How has it begun a Recognition Revolution? What will further fuel it? If you haven't joined the Challenge yet, are you ready to start? Want more inspiration? We will keep refreshing tools too at www.f-r-o-g.ca so keep coming back or sign up to receive updates when we release more tools.

We invite you to connect with us.

As fellow passionate FROGers, we hope you will reach out to us. What questions do you have? What stories can you share with us? What can we celebrate together, and how can we spread that through our network? Reach us on our websites www.greatnessmagnified.com and www.bzmsolutions.com and through social media. We're sincere when we say, we really want to hear from you!

Talk with you soon! FROG on!

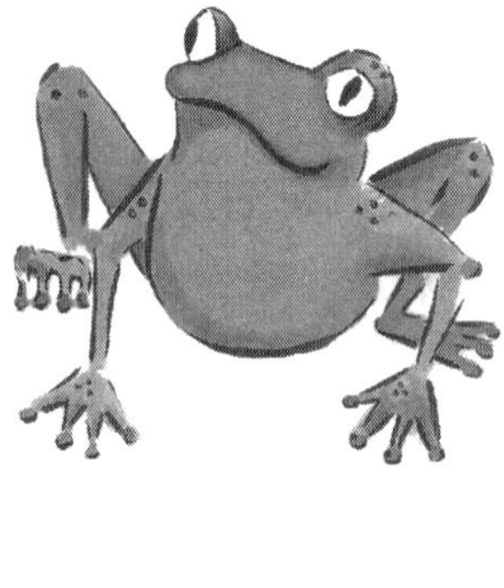

BIOS

Sarah McVanel

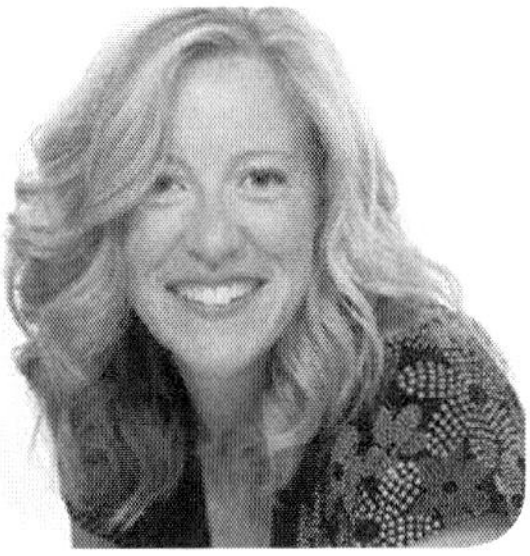

With roots in humanistic psychology, Sarah has spent the last 15 years honing her craft as a coach, professional speaker, facilitator and consultant to help leaders and organizations leverage the power of recognition to increase engagement, retain top talent and improve their bottom lines.

Whether as a senior leader or more recently as the "Chief Recognition Officer" of her own business Greatness Magnified, Sarah helps individuals, teams, and organizations leverage their existing gifts and talents to reach their full potential. She is a certified professional in the fields of human resources, organizational development, and coaching and belongs to the Canadian Association of Professional Speakers. She has been married to her husband Mark for 17 years, and together they secretly study the greatness in her kids, Justin (12) and Simonne (10).

Brenda Zalter-Minden

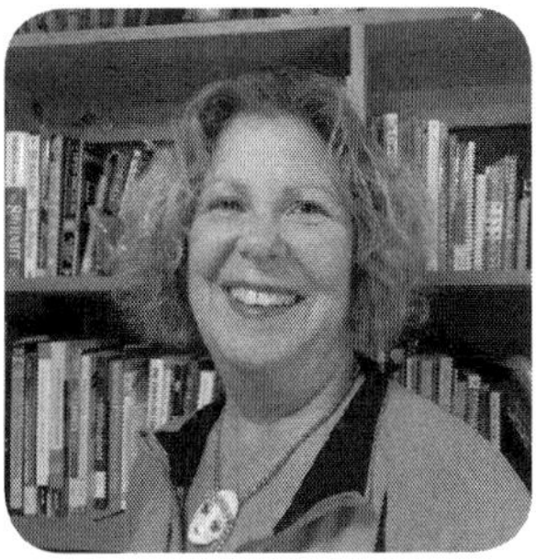

Brenda is the Principal and Founder of BZM Solutions, a business that helps organizations, teams, and individuals flourish utilizing a solution focused approach. Her passion for this line of work grew throughout her ten-year employment in healthcare as an internal consultant. She has gained a wealth of experience over the last twenty-six years in various capacities. Her areas of specialization currently include leadership, management, team building, coaching, facilitating, and creating workshops. Brenda has taught postgraduate students part-time for Toronto Advanced Professional Education (T.A.P.E), Faculty of Social Work, Continuing Education, affiliated with the University of Toronto, as well as for the Adler Learning Centre where she teaches solution focused interventions on a variety of topics. She had the privilege of being trained by both Insoo Kim Berg and Steve de Shazer, the founders of the solution focused model. She has adapted their philosophy and has created FROG - Forever Recognize Others' Greatness™. This unique approach builds on strengths, inspires change, and empowers a continuous improvement culture for both management and staff. At the same time, Brenda enjoys life to the fullest...one day at a time.

BRING FROG INTO YOUR WORKPLACE AND LIFE!

How Sarah Can Help You and Your Organization

1. Grab Some Valuable Resources - For the tools in this book, visit www.f-r-o-g.ca. For even more juicy resources, check out our "Cool Stuff" page at www.greatnessmagnified.com for tools, white papers, infographics and more.

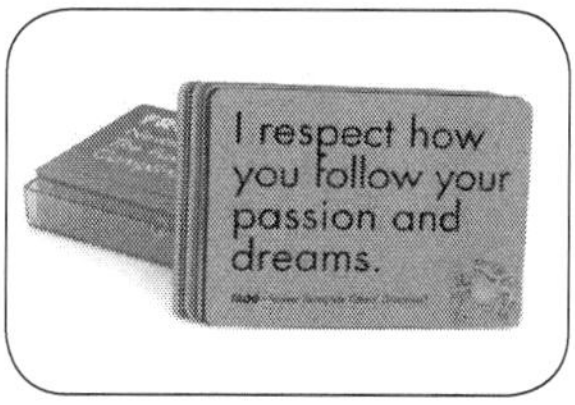

2. Book a Recognition Strategy Session - Need to boost retention, engagement, innovation, and collaboration in your team and organization? Book a strategy session with Sarah through our Contact Page at www.greatnessmagnified.com/contact/

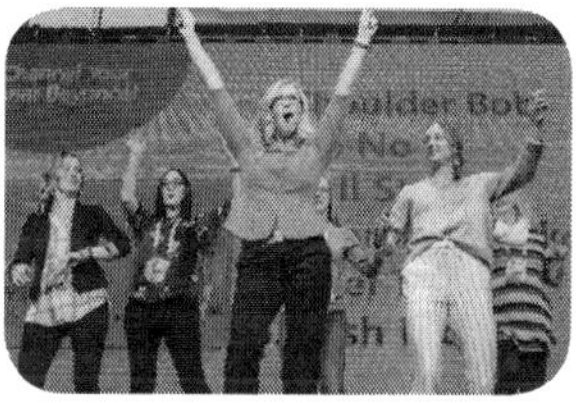

3. Hire Sarah to Speak - Looking to leverage recognition to retain top talent, boost customer satisfaction, and elevate even your own job satisfaction? See all of Sarah's speaking topics at https://greatnessmagnified.com/speaking/ and connect with us anytime at hello@greatnessmagnified.com

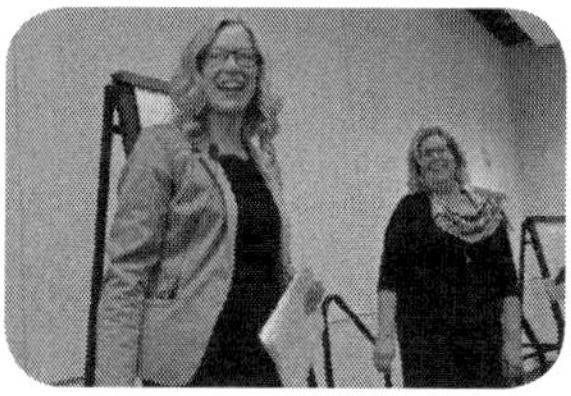

4. Shop for Recognition Tools - Find all of the recognition tools in this book - from solution focused coaching cards to FROG products to compliment cards and more - at www.greatnessmagnified.com/store/. Our Store has an abundance of fun, novel, easy and professional tools to bring recognition into your workplace, home base and community space!

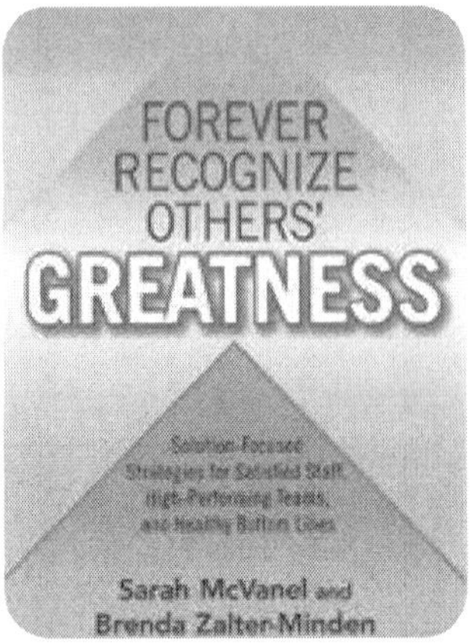

5. (Re)Launch Your Recognition Program - looking for Sarah's best advice about how you can build or relaunch a scrumptious recognition program? Sarah tells you exactly how and provides all of her tools in her virtual program. Learn more by visiting www.greatnessmagnified.com/store/

REFERENCES

Baranowsky, A. B., & Gentry, J. E. (1997). *Compassion Fatigue Resiliency and Recovery: The Accelerated Recovery Program for Compassion Fatigue.* Available at: http://www.tir.org/research_pub/research/compassion_fatigue.html

Bersin, J., Agarwal, D., Pelster, B., & Schwartz, J. (2015). *Global Human Capital Trends 2015: Leading in the New World.* Available at: http://www2. deloitte.com/us/en/pages/human-capital/articles/introduction-human- capital-trends.html

Bridges, W., with Bridges, S. (2009). *Managing Transitions: Making the Most of Change.* Philadelphia: Perseus Books.

Brown, J & Isaacs, D. (2005). *The World Café: Shaping our Futures Through Conversations That Matter.* San Francisco: Berrett-Koehler.

De Jong, P., & Berg, I. K. (2001). *Interviewing for Solutions. 4th ed.* Belmont, CA: Brooks/Cole.

Figley, C. (1995). *Compassion Fatigue: Coping with Secondary Traumatic Stress Disorder in Those Who Treat the Traumatized.* New York: Routledge.

Fiske, H. (2008). *Hope in Action: Solution Focused Conversations About Suicide.* New York: Routledge.

Jackson, P. Z., & McKergow, M. (2011). *The Solutions Focus: Making Coaching and Change Simple.* London: Nicholas Brealey.

McVanel, S. & Zalter-Minden, B. (2015). *Forever Recognize Others' Greatness: Solution Focused Strategies for Satisfied Staff,*

High Performing Teams and Healthy Bottom Lines. Toronto: BPS Publishing.

Nelson, T. (2010). *Doing Something Different: Solution Focused Brief Therapy Practices.* New York: Routledge.

_______ . (2005). *Education and Training in Solution Focused Brief Therapy.* New York: Routledge.

Rohrig, P. & Clarke, J. (2008). *57 Solution Focused Activities for Facilitators and Consultants: Pulling Solutions Focus into Action.* London, England: Solutions Books.

Shaked, D. (2013). *Strength-Based Lean Six Sigma: Building Positive and Engaging Business Improvement.* Philadelphia: Kogan Page.

Shepherd, K. with Sherriff, J. (2010). *The Bite Me School of Management: Taking a Bit Out of Conventional Thinking.* Irvine, CA: Decision Toolbox.

Stavors, J. & Hinrichs, G. (2009). *Thin Book of SOAR: Building Strengths-Based Strategy.* Bend, OR: Thin Book Publishing.

Stubblefield, A. (2004). *The Baptist Health Care Journey to Excellence: Creating a Culture That WOWs!* Hoboken, NJ: John Wiley & Sons.